The Step-By-Step Guide To The

25 Most Common
Microsoft® Excel®

Formulas & Features

C.J. Benton

DEDICATION

To users searching for a concise
Microsoft® Excel® Formulas & Features book!

Other Books Available By This Author:

1. The Step-By-Step Guide To **Pivot Tables** & Introduction To **Dashboards**

2. The Step-By-Step Guide To The **VLOOKUP** formula in Microsoft® Excel®

3. The Microsoft® Excel® Step-By-Step Training Guide Book Bundle

CONTENTS

CONTENTS CONTINUED:

PREFACE

For nearly twenty years, I worked as a Data & Systems Analyst for three different Fortune 500 companies, primarily in the areas of Finance, Infrastructure Services, and Logistics. During that time I used Microsoft® Excel® extensively developing hundreds of different types of reports, analysis tools, and several forms of Dashboards.

I've utilized many Microsoft® Excel® features, including Pivot Tables, VLOOKUP, IF formulas, and much more. The following are the functions and features I used and taught the most to fellow colleagues.

CHAPTER 1
HOW TO USE THIS BOOK

This book can be used as a tutorial or quick reference guide. It is intended for users who are just getting started with the fundamentals of Microsoft® Excel®, as well as for users who understand the basics and now want to build upon this skill by learning the more common intermediate level Excel® formulas and features.

While this book is intended for beginners, it does assume you already know how to create, open, save, and modify an Excel® workbook, and have a general familiarity with the Excel® toolbar.

All of the examples in this book use Microsoft® Excel® 2013, however, most of the functionality and formulas can be applied with Microsoft® Excel® version 2007 or later.

Please always **back-up your work** and **save often**. A good best practice when attempting any new functionality is to **create a copy of the original spreadsheet** and implement your changes on the copied spreadsheet. Should anything go wrong, you then have the original spreadsheet to fall back on. Please see the diagram below.

Diagram 1:

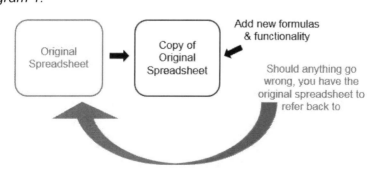

This book was written in the United States, therefore many of the examples use the US dollar currency symbol **$**. For instructions on how to change the currency symbol, for example to the **British Pound £** or **Euro €**, please see chapter 18 'Excel Shortcuts & Tips', page 115.

This book is structured into five parts. Part one focuses on basic formulas. This is where users who are just beginning to learn Excel® would typically start. The next three parts are intended for intermediate level users, they examine the features of Pivot Tables, data sorting, conditional formatting, and supporting formulas that can be used when troubleshooting Pivot Table report results and other spreadsheets. Concluding with part five, which introduces some advanced Excel® functionality of the VLOOKUP, IF, and Nested IF formulas.

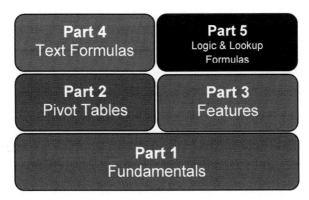

The table below is a summary of the functionality and features detailed in each part:

PART 1 - Fundamentals	
Chapters 2 - 6 10 Formulas	• Sum, Subtraction, Multiplication, & Division • Average, Minimum, & Maximum • Today(), & Networkdays • SumIF
PART 2 - Introduction To Pivot Tables	
Chapter 7 1 Feature	• How to create a basic Pivot Table • Formatting Pivot Table results • Inserting Pivot Charts
PART 3 – Excel® Features	
Chapters 8 - 11 4 Features	• Data Sorting • Formula Trace • Text-To-Columns • Conditional Formatting
PART 4 – Text Functions	
Chapters 12 - 15 7 Formulas	• LEN & TRIM • CONCATENATE & MID • PROPER, UPPER, & LOWER
PART 5 – Logic & Lookup Formulas	
Chapters 16 & 17 3 Formulas	• VLOOKUP (basics) • IF (formula) • Nested IF (formula)

To enhance readability and for those who want to skip to specific areas, each chapter consists of _one or more_ of the following sections:

Diagram 2:

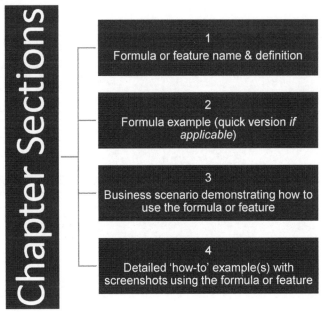

SECTION 1:

Provides the formula or feature name and definition for that chapter.

SECTION 2:

Gives a quick example of how to use the formula and the results. This is intended for intermediate level users who do not require a detailed step-by-step example. Also, this section can be used as a quick reference of the syntax.

SECTION 3:

Offers one or more business scenarios demonstrating how the formula or feature may be used.

SECTION 4:

Presents detailed instructions with screenshots explaining how to answer each chapter's scenario.

(PART 1) - CHAPTER 2
SUM, SUBTRACTION, MULTIPLICATION, & DIVISION

This chapter is intended for users relatively new to Excel®. These are the fundamental formulas that everyone starts with.

FORMULA	OPERATOR	DEFINITION
Sum	+	Adds two or more cells or numbers together
Subtraction	-	Subtracts two or more cells or numbers
Multiplication	*	Multiplies two or more cells or numbers
Division	/	Divides two or more cells or numbers

Detailed examples of how to use each basic formula:

SUM

1. Begin by creating a new blank Excel® spreadsheet

2. Enter the following numbers into **column 'A'**
   a. Cell '**A1**' enter the number **2**
   b. Cell '**A2**' enter the number **3**
   c. Cell '**A3**' enter the number **1**
   d. Cell '**A4**' enter the number **2**

The spreadsheet should look similar to the following:

	A
1	2
2	3
3	1
4	2
5	

3. Click cell **'A5'**

4. From the toolbar select **Formulas**

5. Click **AutoSum**

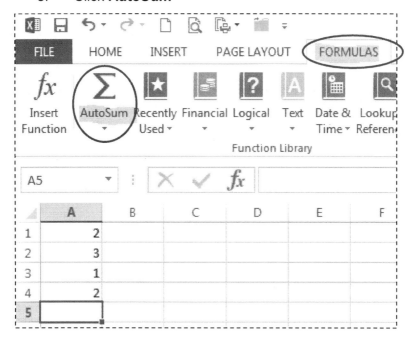

The result should be **8**:

Alternatively, you may also enter the following into cell **'A5'**:

1. Enter the **equal (=)** ⊞ symbol from your keyboard

2. Type **sum(**

3. Highlight rows **'A1-A4'**

4. Press the **'Enter'** button on your keyboard

SUBTRACTION

Using the same the sample data as the 'Sum' section:

1. Start by clicking cell **'B3'**

2. Enter the **equal (=)** symbol from your keyboard

3. Click cell '**A2**'

4. Enter the minus (-) symbol from your keyboard

5. Click cell '**A3**'

6. Press the **'Enter'** button on your keyboard

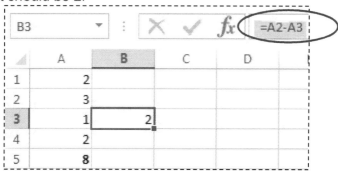

The result should be **2**:

MULTIPLICATION

Using the same the sample data as the 'Sum' section:

1. Start by clicking cell **'B4'**

2. Enter the **equal (=)** symbol from your keyboard

3. Click cell '**A4'**

4. Enter the asterisk (*) symbol from your keyboard

5. Click cell '**A1'**

6. Press the **'Enter'** button on your keyboard

The result should be **4**:

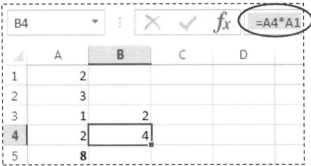

8

DIVISION

Using the same the sample data as the 'Sum' section:

1. Start by clicking cell **'C4'**

2. Enter the **equal (=)** $\boxed{\begin{array}{c}+\\=\end{array}}$ symbol from your keyboard

3. Click cell '**B4'**

4. Enter the backslash (/) $\boxed{\begin{array}{c}?\\/\end{array}}$ symbol from your keyboard

5. Click cell '**B3'**

6. Press the **'Enter'** $\boxed{\begin{array}{c}\text{Enter}\\\leftarrow\end{array}}$ button on your keyboard

◢	A	B	C
1	2		
2	3		
3	1	2	
4	2	4	=B4/B3
5	8		

The result should be **2**:

C4		▼	⋮	✕	✓	*fx*	=B4/B3

◢	A	B	C	D
1	2			
2	3			
3	1	2		
4	2	4	2	
5	8			

(PART 1) - CHAPTER 3
FORMULA = AVERAGE

Formula:
- AVERAGE

Definition:

- Returns the average number in a range of values, does not include text in the evaluation.

Quick Example:

```
Formula Syntax:
AVERAGE(number1, [number2], ...)
Number1 is required, subsequent numbers are optional
```

A4		:	X	✓	*fx*	=AVERAGE(A2:A3)

	A	B	C	D	E
1	SALES				
2	$100				
3	$200				
4	$150				

Scenario:

You have a list of sales numbers and would like to determine the average of all the sales.

Detailed Example How To Use The Formula:

1. Begin by creating a new Excel® spreadsheet

2. Enter the following numbers into **column 'A'**
   a. Cell '**A1**' enter the label '**SALES**'
   b. Cell '**A2**' enter the number **$100**
   c. Cell '**A3**' enter the number **$200**
   d. Cell '**A4**' enter the number **$300**
   e. Cell '**A5**' enter the number **$400**

The spreadsheet should look similar to the following:

	A
1	**SALES**
2	$100
3	$200
4	$300
5	$400

3. Click cell '**A6**'

4. From the toolbar select **Formulas**

5. Click **AutoSum** drop-down box and select '**Average**'

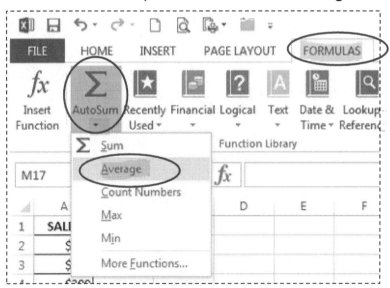

The result should be **250**:

Alternatively, you may also enter the following into cell '**A6**':

1. Enter the **equal [=]** $\boxed{\begin{smallmatrix}+\\=\end{smallmatrix}}$ symbol from your keyboard

2. Type **average(**

3. Highlight rows '**A2 - A5**'

4. Press the '**Enter**' $\boxed{\begin{smallmatrix}\text{Enter}\\ \hookleftarrow\end{smallmatrix}}$ key on your keyboard

You've now determined the average sales from the list above.

(PART 1) - CHAPTER 4
FORMULAS = MIN & MAX

Formulas:
- MIN & MAX

Definition:

- **MIN:** Returns the *lowest number* in a range of values, does not include text in the evaluation.

- **MAX:** Returns the *largest number* in a range of values, does not include text in the evaluation.

Quick Example: MIN

```
Formula Syntax:
MIN(number1, [number2], ...)
Number1 is required, subsequent numbers are optional
```

B2	▾	:	×	✓	fx	=MIN(A2:A6)

◢	A	B	C	D	E
1	LIST	MIN	MAX		
2	1	1			
3	2				
4	3				
5	4				
6	5				

Quick Example: MAX

```
MAX(number1, [number2], ...)
Number1 is required, subsequent numbers are optional
```

| C2 | | ▼ | : | ✕ ✓ f_x | =MAX(A2:A6) |

◢	A	B	C	D	E
1	LIST	MIN	MAX		
2	1	1	5		
3	2				
4	3				
5	4				
6	5				

Scenario:

You've been given a spreadsheet that contains the total fruit sales by quarter and sales person. You've been asked to provide the top and worst performing sales person by quarter.

Detailed Example How To Use The Formula:

Sample data:

	A	B	C	D
1	SALES PERSON FIRST NAME	SALES PERSON LAST NAME	QTR	TOTAL
2	Jack	Smith	1	343
3	Jack	Smith	2	1,849
4	Jack	Smith	3	2,653
5	Jack	Smith	4	5,494
6	Joe	Tanner	1	377
7	Joe	Tanner	2	2,404
8	Joe	Tanner	3	3,980
9	Joe	Tanner	4	39,631
10	Helen	Simpson	1	457
11	Helen	Simpson	2	4,062
12	Helen	Simpson	4	8,954
13	Helen	Simpson	4	20,459
14	Billy	Winchester	1	552
15	Billy	Winchester	2	6,865
16	Billy	Winchester	3	16,558
17	Billy	Winchester	4	8,516

1. Insert three labels:
   a. Cell '**F1**' label '**BEST**'
   b. Cell '**G1**' label '**QTR.**'
   c. Cell '**H1**' label '**SALES**'
   d. Leave two blank rows (rows 2 & 3)

2. Insert three more labels:
   a. Cell '**F4**' label '**WORST**'
   b. Cell '**G4**' label '**QTR.**'
   c. Cell '**H4**' label '**SALES**'
   d. Leave one blank row (row 5)

Please see screenshot below for an example:

	A	B	C	D	E	F	G	H
1	SALES PERSON FIRST NAME	SALES PERSON LAST NAME	QTR	TOTAL		BEST	QTR.	SALES
2	Jack	Smith	1	343				
3	Jack	Smith	2	1,849				
4	Jack	Smith	3	2,653		WORST	QTR.	SALES
5	Jack	Smith	4	5,494				
6	Joe	Tanner	1	377				
7	Joe	Tanner	2	2,404				
8	Joe	Tanner	3	3,980				
9	Joe	Tanner	4	39,631				
10	Helen	Simpson	1	457				
11	Helen	Simpson	2	4,062				
12	Helen	Simpson	4	8,954				
13	Helen	Simpson	4	20,459				
14	Billy	Winchester	1	552				
15	Billy	Winchester	2	6,865				
16	Billy	Winchester	3	16,558				
17	Billy	Winchester	4	8,516				

3. Next, apply the '**MAX**' function for cell '**H2**'

4. From the toolbar select **Formulas : Insert Function**

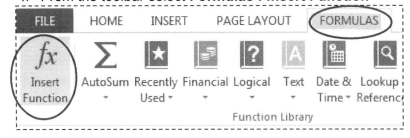

5. Type '**MAX**' in the 'Search for a function:' dialogue box

16

6. Click the '**Go**' button

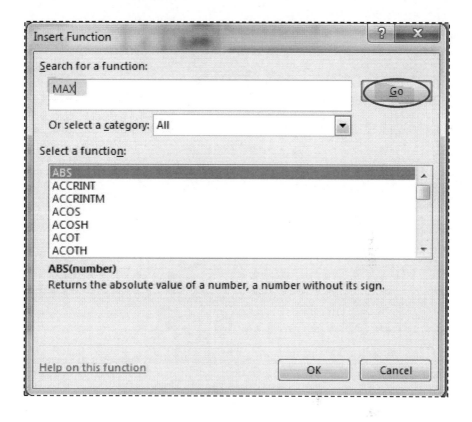

The following dialogue box should now appear:

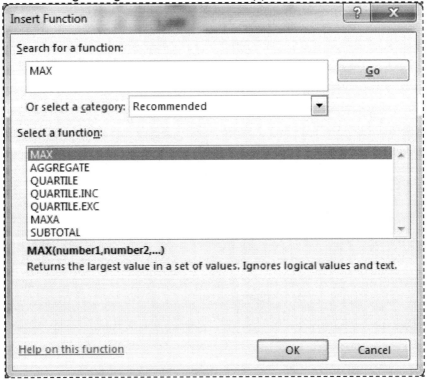

7. Click the '**OK**' button

8. For the **Number1** click the **column 'D'** *(this column lists the sales)*

9. Click the '**OK**' button:

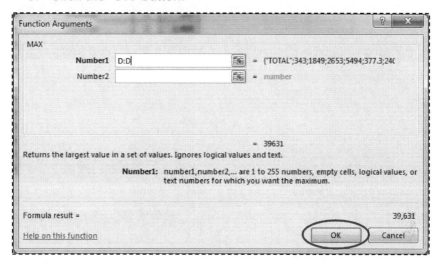

The result is **39,631**:

	A	B	C	D	E	F	G	H
1	SALES PERSON FIRST NAME	SALES PERSON LAST NAME	QTR	TOTAL		BEST	QTR.	SALES
2	Jack	Smith	1	343				39,631
3	Jack	Smith	2	1,849				
4	Jack	Smith	3	2,653		WORST	QTR.	SALES
5	Jack	Smith	4	5,494				
6	Joe	Tanner	1	377				
7	Joe	Tanner	2	2,404				
8	Joe	Tanner	3	3,980				
9	Joe	Tanner	4	39,631				
10	Helen	Simpson	1	457				
11	Helen	Simpson	2	4,062				
12	Helen	Simpson	4	8,954				
13	Helen	Simpson	4	20,459				
14	Billy	Winchester	1	552				
15	Billy	Winchester	2	6,865				
16	Billy	Winchester	3	16,558				
17	Billy	Winchester	4	8,516				

10. Add the last name of the best performing sales person to cell **'F2'** *(Tanner)*

11. Add the quarter to cell **'G2'** *(4)*

12. Repeat steps 4 – 10 above, but instead of using the MAX formula use **MIN** for cell **'H5'**

13. Add the last name of the worst performing sales person to cell **'F5'** *(Smith)*

14. Add the quarter to cell **'G5'** *(1)*

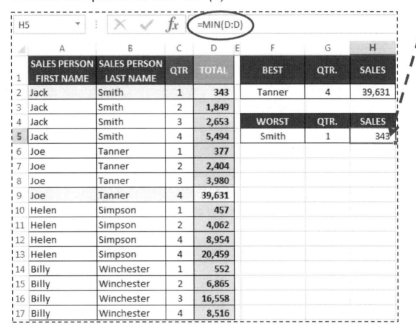

Alternatively, you may also enter the following into cell **'H5'**:

1. Enter the **equal [=]** symbol from your keyboard

2. Type **min(**

3. Highlight column **'D'**

4. Press the **'Enter'** key on your keyboard

or for **MAX**:

You may enter the following into cell **'H2'**:

1.   Enter the **equal [=]** $\boxed{\begin{matrix} + \\ = \end{matrix}}$ symbol from your keyboard
2.   Type **max(**
3.   Highlight column **'D'**

4.   Press the **'Enter'** $\boxed{\begin{matrix} \text{Enter} \\ \leftarrow \end{matrix}}$ key on your keyboard

You've now determined the top and worst performing sales person by quarter.

☑ Additional Information:

All of the formulas reviewed in chapters 2 – 4 can also be accomplished using Pivot Tables, which are introduced in chapter 7. However, sometimes it is quicker to use one of the above formulas when your sample size is small or you're simply providing these results in an email, IM (instant message), or text.

Similarly, these are very useful formulas when you want to quickly double check your Pivot Table results. It's always a good practice to validate your results to ensure you're not missing any values. By taking just a few extra minutes to verify your calculations, you'll likely catch any mistakes, improve your creditability with customers, and have the confidence to defend your work should it ever be questioned.

(PART 1) - CHAPTER 5
FORMULAS = TODAY & NETWORKDAYS

Formulas:
- TODAY
- NETWORKDAYS

Definition:

- **TODAY**: provides today's date. *NOTE: this formula will update each day, it is always the current date.*

- **NETWORKDAYS**: calculates the number of **workdays** (Monday – Friday) between two dates.

Quick Example: TODAY

There is no syntax for the **'Today()'** formula. Alternatively, you may also use the **'Now()'** function, the results would be as follows:

	A	B
1	FORMULA	RESULT
2	=TODAY()	7/13/2015
3	=NOW()	7/13/2015 10:28 AM

Quick Example: NETWORKDAYS

```
Formula Syntax:
NETWORKDAYS(start_date, end_date, [holidays])

start_date and end_date are required, holidays is
optional
```

| C2 | ▾ | ⁝ | ✕ | ✓ | *fx* | =NETWORKDAYS(A2,B2) |

◢	A	B	C	D	E
1	START DATE	COMPLETION DATE	HOW MANY WORKDAYS?		
2	8/1/2015	10/31/2015	65		
3					

Scenario:

You've been asked to determine how many resources are needed to complete a project by specific date.

1. The start of the project is 08/01/2015 and needs to be completed by 10/31/2015
2. The project is estimated to take 1,040 hours
3. Assume each resource would work one 8 hour shift a day, Monday – Friday

It would take 1 resource 130 days to complete the project including weekends:

$$(1040 \text{ hours } / \text{ 8 hour shift } = \text{ 130 days})$$

Therefore we know we need more resources, but how many?

Detailed Example How To Use The Formula:

First, we need to determine how many *workdays* there are between 08/01/2015 and 10/31/2015. Once we know this amount, we can then multiply this value with the number of hours per shift to determine the appropriate total of resources needed to complete the project by 10/31/2015.

1. Begin by creating a new Excel® spreadsheet

2. Enter the following:
   a. Cell '**A1**' enter the label '**START DATE**'
   b. Cell '**A2**' enter the date '**8/1/2015**'
   c. Cell '**B1**' enter the label '**COMPLETION DATE**'
   d. Cell '**B2**' enter the date '**10/31/2015**'
   e. Cell '**C1**' enter the label '**HOW MANY WORKDAYS?**'

3. Place your cursor in cell '**C2**':

	A	B	C
1	START DATE	COMPLETION DATE	HOW MANY WORKDAYS?
2	8/1/2015	10/31/2015	
3			
4			

4. From the toolbar select **Formulas : Insert Function**

5. Type "**NETWORKDAYS**" in the **'Search for a function:'** dialogue box

6. Click the '**Go**' button

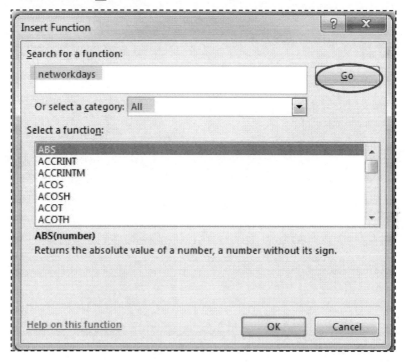

The following dialogue box should now appear:

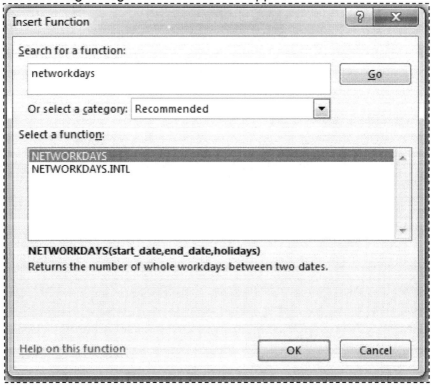

7. Click the 'OK' button:

8. For the **Start_date** click cell '**A2**' or enter **A2**

9. For the **End_date** click cell '**B2**' or enter **B2**

10. Click the '**OK**' button

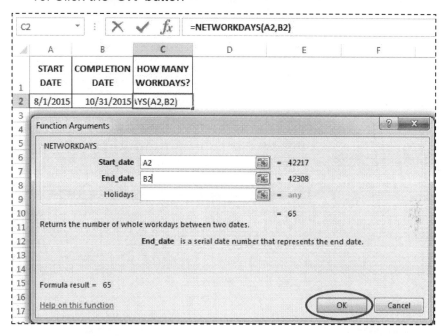

The result is **65 days:**

11. Next, we apply the basic calculations to determine the appropriate amount of resources needed to complete the project (please see screenshot below)

	A	B	C	D	E	F
1	START DATE	COMPLETION DATE	HOW MANY WORKDAYS?	NUMBER OF HOURS WORKED FOR 1 RESOURCE FOR 65 DAYS	ESTIMATED PROJECT HOURS	RESOURCES NEEDED TO COMPLETE BY 10/31/2015
2	8/1/2015	10/31/2015	65	520	1,040	2
3	Formulas used in the above cell			C2*8 = 520		E2/D2 = 2
4						
5						

The result is **2 resources** are needed to complete a project by 10/31/2015.

FORMULAS = SUMIF

Formula:
- SUMIF

Definition:
- Sums the values in a range based on the criteria you identify.

Quick Example:

```
Formula Syntax:
SUMIF(range, criteria, [sum_range])
range and criteria are required, sum_range is
optional
```

F2	▼	:	✕ ✓ fx	=SUMIF(B2:B13,1,C2:C13)

◢	A	B	C	D	E	F	G
1	REGION	QUARTER	APPLES SALES		QUARTER	APPLE SALES	
2	Central	1	111		Q1	751	
3	Central	2	161				
4	Central	3	183				
5	Central	4	243				
6	East	1	263				
7	East	2	313				
8	East	3	335				
9	East	4	395				
10	West	1	377				
11	West	2	427				
12	West	3	449				
13	West	4	509				

Scenario:

You've been given a spreadsheet that contains the Apple sales by quarter for three regions. You've been asked to summarize the data and provide the total apples by quarter.

Detailed Example How To Use The Formula:

Sample data:

	A	B	C
1	REGION	QUARTER	APPLES SALES
2	Central	1	111
3	Central	2	161
4	Central	3	183
5	Central	4	243
6	East	1	263
7	East	2	313
8	East	3	335
9	East	4	395
10	West	1	377
11	West	2	427
12	West	3	449
13	West	4	509

1. Add two columns:
   a. Cell 'E1' label 'QUARTER'
   b. Cell 'F1' label 'APPLE SALES'
   c. Add rows for Quarters Q1 – Q4

See below screenshot for an example:

	A	B	C	D	E	F
1	**REGION**	**QUARTER**	**APPLES SALES**		**QUARTER**	**APPLE SALES**
2	Central	1	111		Q1	
3	Central	2	161		Q2	
4	Central	3	183		Q3	
5	Central	4	243		Q4	
6	East	1	263			
7	East	2	313			
8	East	3	335			
9	East	4	395			
10	West	1	377			
11	West	2	427			
12	West	3	449			
13	West	4	509			

2. Next, apply the '**SUMIF**' function for 'Apple Sales' in row '**F2**'

3. From the toolbar select **Formulas : Insert Function**

4. Type '**SUMIF**' in the '**Search for a function:**' dialogue box
5. Click the '**Go**' button

The following dialogue box should now appear:

6. Click the '**OK**' button:

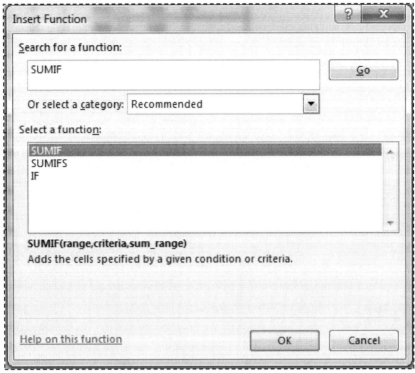

7. For the **Range** click the **column 'B'** *(this column lists the quarter)*

8. For the **Criteria** enter **'1'** for Quarter 1 *(note: if this were a text field, you would encapsulate the text with double quotes " ")*

9. For the **Sum_Range** click the **column 'C'** *(this column list the apple sales)*

10. Click the '**OK**' button:

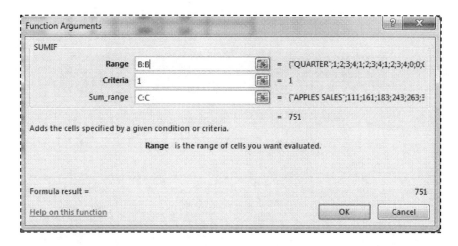

The result for **Q1** is **751** sales:

	A	B	C	D	E	F
					F2	=SUMIF(B:B,1,C:C)
1	REGION	QUARTER	APPLES SALES		QUARTER	APPLE SALES
2	Central	1	111		Q1	751
3	Central	2	161		Q2	
4	Central	3	183		Q3	
5	Central	4	243		Q4	
6	East	1	263			
7	East	2	313			
8	East	3	335			
9	East	4	395			
10	West	1	377			
11	West	2	427			
12	West	3	449			
13	West	4	509			

11. From here, we can copy the formula down through cells **'F3'** – **'F5'** and change the **'Criteria'** value for the appropriate quarter *(i.e. **2,3, & 4 for quarters 2-4**)*.

| SUMIF | ▼ | ⋮ | ✕ | ✓ | *fx* | =SUMIF(B:B,4,C:C) |

	A	B	C	D	E SUMIF(range, crite
1	REGION	QUARTER	APPLES SALES		QUARTER	APPLE SALES
2	Central	1	111		Q1	751
3	Central	2	161		Q2	901
4	Central	3	183		Q3	967
5	Central	4	243		Q4	MIF(B:B,4,C
6	East	1	263			
7	East	2	313			
8	East	3	335			
9	East	4	395			
10	West	1	377			
11	West	2	427			
12	West	3	449			
13	West	4	509			

☑ Additional Information:

In addition to SUMIF, the formulas of COUNTIF, and AVERAGEIF *(please see below for definitions)* can also be accomplished with Pivot Tables, which are introduced in the next chapter. However, sometimes it is quicker to use one of these formulas when your sample size is small or you're simply providing these results in an email, IM (instant message), or text.

COUNTIF: Counts the number of times a values appears in a range of cells based on the criteria you identify.

AVERAGEIF: Returns the average value (number) in a range of cells based on the criteria you identify.

INTRODUCTION TO PIVOT TABLES

Feature:
* Pivot Tables

Definition:
* By using built-in filters and functions, Pivot Tables allow you to quickly organize and summarize large amounts of data. Various types of analysis can then be completed without needing to manually enter formulas into the spreadsheet you're analyzing.

Scenario:

You may be tasked with analyzing significant amounts of data, perhaps consisting of several thousand or hundreds of thousands of records, or you may have to reconcile information from many different sources and forms, such as assimilating material from:

1. Reports generated by another application, such as a legacy system
2. Data imported into Excel® via a query from a database or other application
3. Data copied or cut, and pasted into Excel® from the web or other types of screen scraping activities

One of the easiest ways to perform high level analysis on this information is to use Pivot Tables. The following examples will demonstrate two types of analysis that can be performed on large amounts of data using the Microsoft® Excel® Pivot Table feature. In the following examples we will:

1. Determine the total sales by region and quarter
2. Create a chart that displays the sales by region and quarter

Sample data:

	A	B	C
1	REGION	QUARTER	TOTAL
2	Central	1	5,620
3	Central	2	8,711
4	Central	3	9,379
5	Central	4	14,069
6	East	1	6,109
7	East	2	9,933
8	East	3	14,899
9	East	4	21,539
10	West	1	6,865
11	West	2	13,431
12	West	3	16,558
13	West	4	31,711

Detailed Example How To Use The Feature:

Let's first determine the '**Total Sales by Region**' and then we will build upon this by adding the '**Quarterly Sales by Region**':

1. Select **columns 'A' – 'C'**

2. From the toolbar select **INSERT : PivotTable**

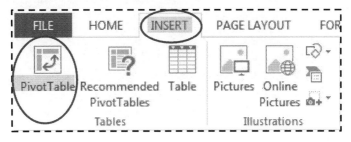

The following dialogue box should appear:

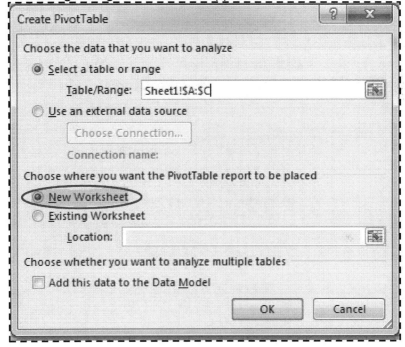

3. For this exercise, select the '**New Worksheet**' radio button

4. Click the '**OK**' button

A new tab will be created and looks similar to the following *(due to display limitations the below screenshot is split, showing the left & right sides of your screen separately)*:

Left side of your screen:

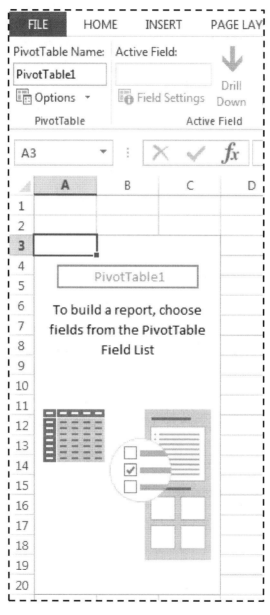

Right side of your screen:

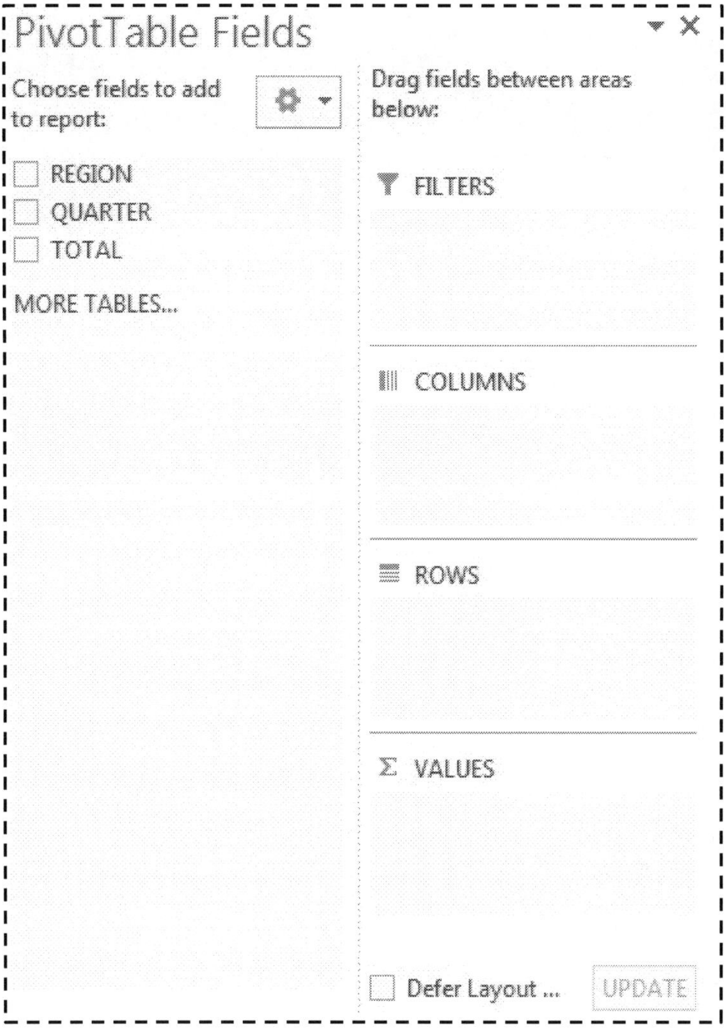

PivotTable Fields ▾ ✕

Choose fields to add to report: ⚙ ▾

Drag fields between areas below:

☐ REGION
☐ QUARTER
☐ TOTAL

MORE TABLES...

▼ FILTERS

⫿⫿⫿ COLUMNS

☰ ROWS

Σ VALUES

☐ Defer Layout ... UPDATE

5. Click the **'REGION'** and **'TOTAL'** check boxes in the **PivotTable Fields** list

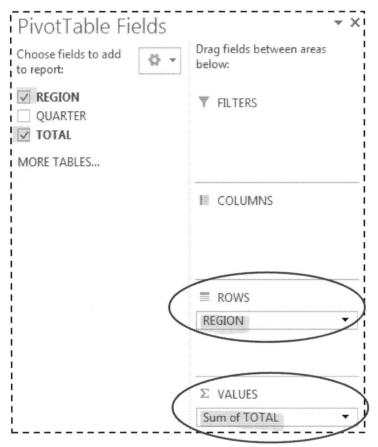

The following should be displayed on the left side of your screen.
Note: *the format is not very easy to read:*

	A	B
1		
2		
3	Row Labels ▼	Sum of TOTAL
4	Central	37778.8125
5	East	52479.6534
6	West	68565.34116
7	(blank)	
8	Grand Total	158823.8071

6. We can change the column labels and format of the numbers. In the below example:

   a. Cell label '**A3**' was changed to '**REGIONS**'

   b. Cell label '**B3**' was changed to '**TOTAL SALES**'

   c. The dollar sales total format was changed to currency with zero decimal places

Below is the formatted example:

	A	B
1		
2		
3	REGIONS ▼	TOTAL SALES
4	Central	$37,779
5	East	$52,480
6	West	$68,565
7	(blank)	
8	Grand Total	$158,824

7. Now let's add the **'QUARTER'** by clicking the check box labeled **'QUARTER'** from the **PivotTable Fields** list. *Note: you may also drag the field 'QUARTER' over to the 'COLUMNS' section of the PivotTable Fields list*

We now have **'QUARTER'** added to the summary

Before *formatting:*

⯅	A	B	C	D	E	F	G
1							
2							
3	TOTAL SALES	Column Labels ▾					
4	REGIONS ▾		1	2	3	4 (blank)	Grand Total
5	Central		$5,620	$8,711	$9,379	$14,069	$37,779
6	East		$6,109	$9,933	$14,899	$21,539	$52,480
7	West		$6,865	$13,431	$16,558	$31,711	$68,565
8	(blank)						
9	Grand Total		$18,594	$32,074	$40,836	$67,319	$158,824

8. Change the label for cell **'B3'** to **'BY QUARTER'**

9. Change the labels for cells **'B4'**, **'C4'**, **'D4'**, & **'E4'** to add the abbreviation '**QTR**' in front of each quarter number

After *formatting:*

⯅	A	B	C	D	E	F	G
1							
2							
3	TOTAL SALES	BY QUARTER ▾					
4	REGIONS ▾	QTR 1	QTR 2	QTR 3	QTR 4	(blank)	Grand Total
5	Central	$5,620	$8,711	$9,379	$14,069		$37,779
6	East	$6,109	$9,933	$14,899	$21,539		$52,480
7	West	$6,865	$13,431	$16,558	$31,711		$68,565
8	(blank)						
9	Grand Total	$18,594	$32,074	$40,836	$67,319		$158,824

Now that we have determined the '**Total Sales by Region**' and the '**Quarterly Sales by Region,**' let's add a chart to the summary

1. From the PIVOTTABLE TOOLS toolbar select the tab
   ANALYZE : PivotChart

<u>Note:</u> *If you do not see the PIVOTTABLE TOOLS option on your toolbar, click any PivotTable cell. This toolbar option only appears when a PivotTable field is active.*

The following dialogue box should appear:

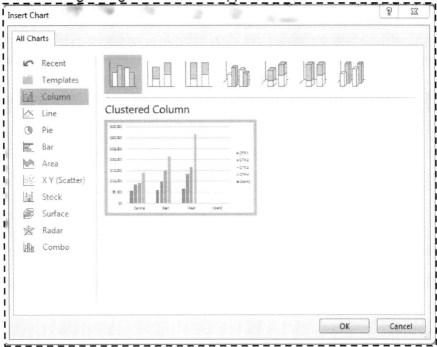

2. Click the **'OK'** button

A chart similar to the below should now be displayed:

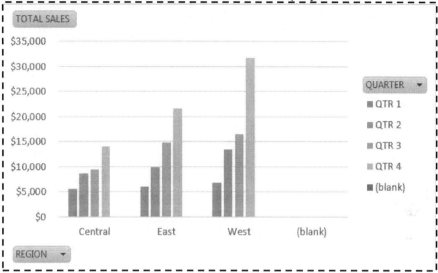

If you would like to learn more about Pivot Tables, please check out my book: The Step-By-Step Guide To Pivot Tables & Introduction To Dashboards

The book contains several basic, intermediate, and advanced Pivot Table examples with screenshots demonstrating how to:

- Organize and summarize data
- Format results
- Inserting both bar and pie Pivot Charts
- Displaying averages & percentages
- Grouping data into predefined ranges
- Ranking results
- Inserting calculated fields

In addition to the above, you will also learn **how to create and update a basic Dashboard** using Pivot Table data.

FEATURE = DATA SORTING

Feature:
- Data Sorting

Definition:
- Allows you to change the order of rows in a spreadsheet to either <u>ascending</u> (A – Z alphabetical) or <u>descending</u> (Z-A reverse alphabetical).

Scenario:

You have a spreadsheet that contains the first and last name of sales associates. You would like to sort this list in alphabetical order by last name.

Detailed Example How To Use The Feature:

1. Begin by creating a new Excel® spreadsheet

2. Enter the following into **columns 'A' & 'B'**
   a. Cell 'A1' enter **'FIRST NAME'** and cell **'B1'** enter **'LAST NAME'**
   b. Cell 'A2' enter **'Helen'** and cell **'B2'** enter **'Smith'**
   c. Cell 'A3' enter **'Jill'** and cell **'B3'** enter **'Johnson'**
   d. Cell 'A4' enter **'Sally'** and cell **'B4'** enter **'Morton'**
   e. Cell 'A5' enter **'John'** and cell **'B5'** enter **'Dower'**
   f. Cell 'A6' enter **'Billy'** and cell **'B6'** enter **'Winchester'**

The spreadsheet should look similar to the following:

	A	B
1	FIRST NAME	LAST NAME
2	Helen	Smith
3	Jill	Johnson
4	Sally	Morton
5	John	Dower
6	Billy	Winchester

3. Highlight columns 'A' & 'B'

4. From the toolbar select **Data : Sort**

The following dialogue box should appear:

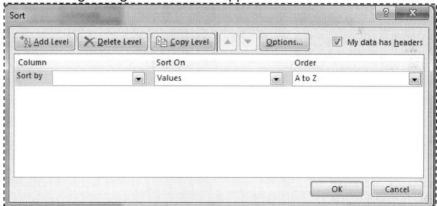

5. In the **'Sort by'** drop-down box select **'LAST NAME'** (this is the _primary_ sort). For the **'Order'** drop-down box select **'A to Z'**

6. Click the **'Add Level'** button, a new row called **'Then by'** will appear

7. In the **'Then by'** drop-down box select **'FIRST NAME'** (this is the _secondary_ sort). For the **'Order'** drop-down box select **'A to Z'**

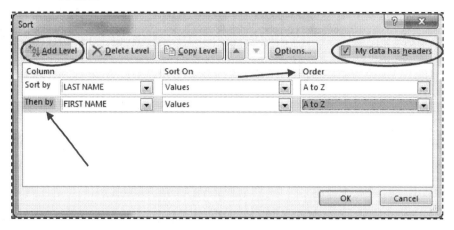

The results should look similar to the following:

	A	B
1	**FIRST NAME**	**LAST NAME**
2	John	Dower
3	Jill	Johnson
4	Sally	Morton
5	Helen	Smith
6	Billy	Winchester

You now have a list in alphabetical order by last name.

Additional Information:

NOTE: the check box **'My data has <u>h</u>eaders.'** Excel allows you to sort any range of cells. If this check box is unselected the **'Sort by'** drop-down options will appear as:

- Column A
- Column B
- Etc.

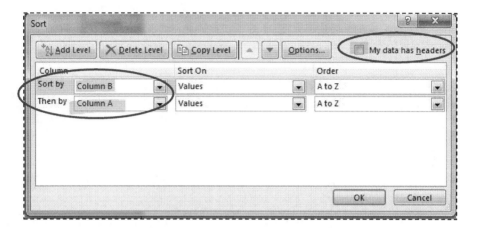

Result if **Order** (primary sort) was **descending (Z to A):**

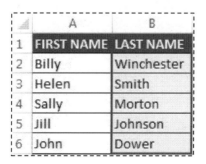

Feature:

- Formula trace is a graphical tool that can either identify all of the cells a formula is referencing *or* displays all the formulas that are dependent on a specific formula (cell).

Definition:

- **Trace Precedents:** Traces and displays graphically, with blue arrows, all of the cells a formula *is referencing.*

- **Trace Dependents:** Traces and displays graphically, with blue arrows, all of the formulas that are *dependent on* it for their calculation.

Quick Example: Trace Precedents

The formula in cell **'B3'** is *referencing values* in **cells 'A2', 'A4',** & **'A5'**:

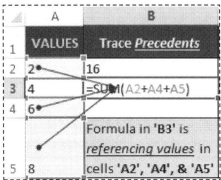

Quick Example: Trace Dependents

The formula in cell **'C3'** is _dependent_ on the formula in **'B3'**:

	A	B	C
1	VALUES	Trace _Precedents_	Trace _Dependents_
2	2	16	20
3	4	=SUM(A2+A4+A5)	=B3*A3
4	6		
5	8		Formula in **'C3'** is _dependent on_ the formula in **'B3'**

Scenario:

The formula trace features within Excel® are an extremely helpful tool when you need to troubleshoot or validate a formula is calculating correctly, especially when troubleshooting complex formulas referencing many cells. Let's walk through a couple of examples:

1. You've been contacted by a sales person who believes his sales are understated. He has asked you to verify his numbers are correct.

2. One of the formulas in a spreadsheet contains the error '#VALUE'. You've been asked to troubleshoot and fix the problem.

3. A report used by sales managers has become increasingly difficult to read. You've been asked if there are some sections that can be deleted. In order to do this without breaking (effecting) other formulas, you decide to use the Trace Dependents feature to ensure removing a particular section does not inadvertently effect other formulas.

Detailed Example How To Use The Feature:

Sample data:

	A	B	D	H	I	J
1	SALES PERSON FIRST NAME	SALES PERSON LAST NAME	QUARTER	TOTAL		B. Winchester
2	Jack	Smith	1	$ 343		63,606
3	Joe	Tanner	1	$ 377		
4	Peter	Graham	1	$ 415		
5	Helen	Simpson	1	$ 457		
6	Alex	Steller	1	$ 502		
7	Billy	Winchester	1	$ 552		
8	Jack	Smith	2	$ 1,849		
9	Joe	Tanner	2	$ 2,404		
10	Peter	Graham	2	$ 3,125		
11	Helen	Simpson	2	$ 4,062		
12	Alex	Steller	2	$ 5,281		
13	Billy	Winchester	2	$ 6,865		
14	Jack	Smith	3	$ 2,653		
15	Joe	Tanner	3	$ 3,980		
16	Peter	Graham	3	$ 5,969		
17	Alex	Steller	3	$ 13,431		
18	Billy	Winchester	3	$ 16,558		
19	Jack	Smith	4	$ 5,494		
20	Joe	Tanner	4	$ 8,516		
21	Billy	Winchester	4	$ 39,631		
22	Peter	Graham	4	$ 13,199		
23	Helen	Simpson	4	$ 8,954		
24	Alex	Steller	4	$ 31,711		

The sales person Billy Winchester has asked you to verify his sales numbers are correct for the year.

1. Place your cursor in cell '**J2**'

2. From the toolbar select **Formulas : Trace Precedents**

A similar type of graphic should appear:

J2	▼	:	✕	✓	fx	=SUM(H7+H13+H18+H21)

	A	B	D	H	I	J
1	SALES PERSON FIRST NAME	SALES PERSON LAST NAME	QUARTER	TOTAL		B. Winchester
2	Jack	Smith	1	$ 343		63,606
3	Joe	Tanner	1	$ 377		
4	Peter	Graham	1	$ 415		
5	Helen	Simpson	1	$ 457		
6	Alex	Steller	1	$ 502		
7	Billy	Winchester	1	$ 552		
8	Jack	Smith	2	$ 1,849		
9	Joe	Tanner	2	$ 2,404		
10	Peter	Graham	2	$ 3,125		
11	Helen	Simpson	2	$ 4,062		
12	Alex	Steller	2	$ 5,281		
13	Billy	Winchester	2	$ 6,865		
14	Jack	Smith	3	$ 2,653		
15	Joe	Tanner	3	$ 3,980		
16	Peter	Graham	3	$ 5,969		
17	Alex	Steller	3	$ 13,431		
18	Billy	Winchester	3	$ 16,558		
19	Jack	Smith	4	$ 5,494		
20	Joe	Tanner	4	$ 8,516		
21	Billy	Winchester	4	$ 39,631		
22	Peter	Graham	4	$ 13,199		
23	Helen	Simpson	4	$ 8,954		
24	Alex	Steller	4	$ 31,711		

We've now verified the sales for Billy Winchester are correct for the year.

Now, let's look at how Trace Precedents can help us troubleshoot a formula that contains an error.

Sample data:

	A	B	C	D	E	F	G	H	I
1	SALES PERSON FIRST NAME	SALES PERSON LAST NAME	QUARTER	TOTAL		Q1	Q2	Q3	Q4
2	Peter	Graham	1	$ 415		$ 2,646	#VALUE!	$ 49,375	$ 107,505
3	Peter	Graham	2	$ 3,125					
4	Peter	Graham	3	$ 5,969					
5	Peter	Graham	4	$ 13,199					
6	Helen	Simpson	1	$ 457					
7	Helen	Simpson	2	$ 4,062					
8	Helen	Simpson	3	$ 6,785					
9	Helen	Simpson	4	$ 8,954					
10	Jack	Smith	1	$ 343					
11	Jack	Smith	2	$ 1,849					
12	Jack	Smith	3	$ 2,653					
13	Jack	Smith	4	$ 5,494					
14	Alex	Steller	1	$ 502					
15	Alex	Steller	2	$ 5,281					
16	Alex	Steller	3	$ 13,431					
17	Alex	Steller	4	$ 31,711					
18	Joe	Tanner	1	$ 377					
19	Joe	Tanner	2	$ 2403.7					
20	Joe	Tanner	3	$ 3,980					
21	Joe	Tanner	4	$ 8,516					
22	Billy	Winchester	1	$ 552					
23	Billy	Winchester	2	$ 6,865					
24	Billy	Winchester	3	$ 16,558					
25	Billy	Winchester	4	$ 39,631					

1. Place your cursor in cell **'G2'**

2. From the toolbar select **Formulas : Trace Precedents**

A similar type of graphic will be displayed. It appears someone has inadvertently typed the letter 'O', instead of the number zero (**0**) in cell **'D19'**.

| G2 | ▾ | ⁞ | ✕ ✓ *fx* | =SUM(D3+D7+D11+D15+D19+D23) |

	A	B	C	D	E	F	G	H	I
1	SALES PERSON FIRST NAME	SALES PERSON LAST NAME	QUARTER	TOTAL		Q1	Q2	Q3	Q4
2	Peter	Graham	1	$ 415		$ 2,646	#VALUE!	$ 49,375	$ 107,505
3	Peter	Graham	2	$ 3,125					
4	Peter	Graham	3	$ 5,969					
5	Peter	Graham	4	$ 13,199					
6	Helen	Simpson	1	$ 457					
7	Helen	Simpson	2	$ 4,062					
8	Helen	Simpson	3	$ 6,785					
9	Helen	Simpson	4	$ 8,954					
10	Jack	Smith	1	$ 343					
11	Jack	Smith	2	$ 1,849					
12	Jack	Smith	3	$ 2,653					
13	Jack	Smith	4	$ 5,494					
14	Alex	Steller	1	$ 502					
15	Alex	Steller	2	$ 5,281					
16	Alex	Steller	3	$ 13,431					
17	Alex	Steller	4	$ 31,711					
18	Joe	Tanner	1	$ 377					
19	Joe	Tanner	2	$ 24O3.7					
20	Joe	Tanner	3	$ 3,980					
21	Joe	Tanner	4	$ 8,516					
22	Billy	Winchester	1	$ 552					
23	Billy	Winchester	2	$ 6,865					
24	Billy	Winchester	3	$ 16,558					
25	Billy	Winchester	4	$ 39,631					

3. To fix, remove the letter **'O'** and replace with the number zero **(0)** in cell **'D19'**.

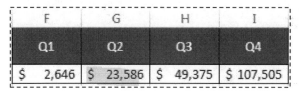

F	G	H	I
Q1	Q2	Q3	Q4
$ 2,646	$ 23,586	$ 49,375	$ 107,505

A report used by sales managers has become increasingly difficult to read They've asked you if the *'CURRENT YR' sales section* can be removed? You decide to use the **Trace Dependents** feature to ensure removing this particular section does not inadvertently effect other formulas.

Current report:

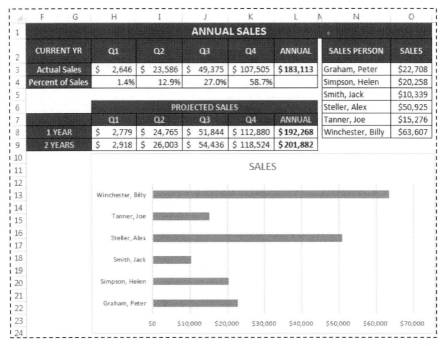

1. Place your cursor in cell **'H3'**

2. From the toolbar select **Formulas : Trace Dependents**

A similar type of graphic will be displayed. We can see that cells **'H4'** & **'H8'** are *dependent* on cell **'H3'** which is part of the *'CURRENT YR' sales section*. Therefore, if you were to remove this section it would adversely affect other formulas is this spreadsheet.

	F	G	H	I	J	K	L	M
1				ANNUAL SALES				
2	CURRENT YR		Q1	Q2	Q3	Q4	ANNUAL	
3	Actual Sales		$ 2,646	$ 23,586	$ 49,375	$ 107,505	$183,113	
4	Percent of Sales		1.4%	12.9%	27.0%	58.7%		
5								
6				PROJECTED SALES				
7			Q1	Q2	Q3	Q4	ANNUAL	
8	1 YEAR		$ 2,779	$ 24,765	$ 51,844	$ 112,880	$192,268	
9	2 YEARS		$ 2,918	$ 26,003	$ 54,436	$ 118,524	$201,882	

To remove the arrows, there are two options:

    A. From the toolbar select **Formulas : Remove Arrows** <u>*or*</u>

    B. **Save** the spreadsheet

(PART 3) - CHAPTER 10
FEATURE = TEXT TO COLUMNS

Feature:
- Text To Columns

Definition:
- Allows you to parse merged data from a single cell, fixed width, delimited, or structured file into separate Excel® columns.

Scenario:
One of the things I've often had to do in my career is parse information given to me from a source that has merged data elements together.

Some of the most common examples are:

1. Reports generated by another application *(often legacy systems)*. These reports are typically created in a **text (.txt)** or **comma separated file (.CSV)**.

2. Data exported by a query from a database or other applications and pasted into Excel®.

3. Data copied or cut, and pasted into Excel® from the web or other types of screen scraping activities.

Detailed Example How To Use The Feature:

Let's walk through an example of data pasted into Excel®. The data elements are merged into a single cell (column **'A'**) and are separated by a comma.

Sample data:

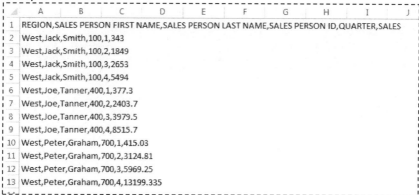

	A	B	C	D	E	F	G	H	I	J
1	REGION,SALES PERSON FIRST NAME,SALES PERSON LAST NAME,SALES PERSON ID,QUARTER,SALES
2	West,Jack,Smith,100,1,343
3	West,Jack,Smith,100,2,1849
4	West,Jack,Smith,100,3,2653
5	West,Jack,Smith,100,4,5494
6	West,Joe,Tanner,400,1,377.3
7	West,Joe,Tanner,400,2,2403.7
8	West,Joe,Tanner,400,3,3979.5
9	West,Joe,Tanner,400,4,8515.7
10	West,Peter,Graham,700,1,415.03
11	West,Peter,Graham,700,2,3124.81
12	West,Peter,Graham,700,3,5969.25
13	West,Peter,Graham,700,4,13199.335

1. Click on **column 'A'**, make sure the entire column is highlighted

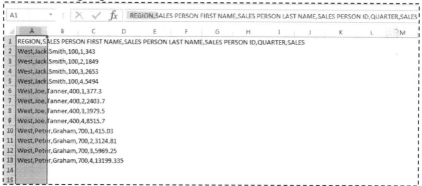

2. From the toolbar select **DATA : Text to Columns**

The following dialogue box / Wizard should appear:

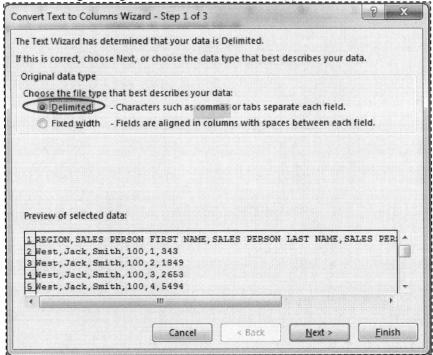

3. Select the '**Delimited**' radio button and click the '**Next>**' button

The following dialogue box should appear:

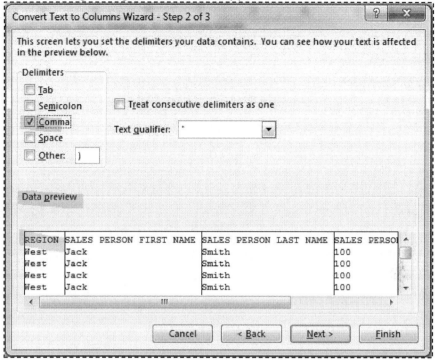

4. Select the '**Comma**' check box as your delimiter. **Note** the '**Data preview**' section. *There are now separate columns of the what was the merged data in column 'A'*

5. If the data appears to be parsed correctly, click the '**Finish**' button

The merged data is now parsed into separate columns:

	A	B	C	D	E	F
1	REGION	SALES PERSON FIRST NAME	SALES PERSON LAST NAME	SALES PERSON ID	QUARTER	SALES
2	West	Jack	Smith	100	1	343
3	West	Jack	Smith	100	2	1849
4	West	Jack	Smith	100	3	2653
5	West	Jack	Smith	100	4	5494
6	West	Joe	Tanner	400	1	377.3
7	West	Joe	Tanner	400	2	2403.7
8	West	Joe	Tanner	400	3	3979.5
9	West	Joe	Tanner	400	4	8515.7
10	West	Peter	Graham	700	1	415.03
11	West	Peter	Graham	700	2	3124.81
12	West	Peter	Graham	700	3	5969.25
13	West	Peter	Graham	700	4	13199.335

FEATURE = CONDITIONAL FORMATTING

Feature:
- Conditional Formatting

Definition:
- Using different colors for cell shading and fonts, Conditional Formatting allows you to highlight cells based on specific criteria.

- Preset options include:
    - The Top & Bottom 10 *(the number 10 can be adjusted)*
    - The Top & Bottom 10% *(this percentage can also be adjusted)*
    - Above & Below the Average

- A very useful tool to quickly identify:
    - Duplicate values
    - A reoccurring date
    - Values greater or less than a specific number
    - Equal to a specific number
    - Cells that contain specific text

Scenario:

You've been given a spreadsheet that contains the total fruit sales by quarter and sales person. You've been asked to provide the *sales people* and *quarter* in which:

- Sales are greater than $10,000
- Sales are less than $1,000

Detailed Example How To Use The Feature:

Sample data:

	A	B	C	D
1	SALES PERSON FIRST NAME	SALES PERSON LAST NAME	QUARTER	TOTAL
2	Jack	Smith	1	$ 343
3	Jack	Smith	2	$ 1,849
4	Jack	Smith	3	$ 2,653
5	Jack	Smith	4	$ 5,494
6	Joe	Tanner	1	$ 377
7	Joe	Tanner	2	$ 2,404
8	Joe	Tanner	3	$ 3,980
9	Joe	Tanner	4	$ 39,631
10	Peter	Graham	1	$ 415
11	Peter	Graham	2	$ 3,125
12	Peter	Graham	3	$ 5,969
13	Peter	Graham	4	$ 13,199
14	Helen	Simpson	1	$ 457
15	Helen	Simpson	2	$ 4,062
16	Helen	Simpson	4	$ 8,954
17	Helen	Simpson	4	$ 20,459
18	Alex	Steller	1	$ 502
19	Alex	Steller	2	$ 5,281
20	Alex	Steller	3	$ 13,431
21	Alex	Steller	4	$ 31,711
22	Billy	Winchester	1	$ 552
23	Billy	Winchester	2	$ 6,865
24	Billy	Winchester	3	$ 16,558
25	Billy	Winchester	4	$ 8,516

1. Highlight cells 'D2 – D25'

2. From the toolbar select **HOME : Conditional Formatting**

3. Select <u>**Highlight Cells Rules > Greater Than...**</u>

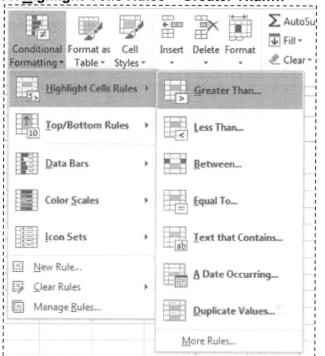

The following dialogue box should appear:

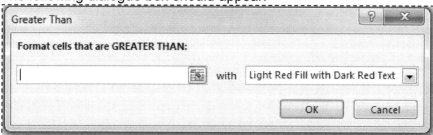

4. In the **'Format cells that are GREATER THAN':** box enter **$10,000**

5. In the **'with'** box, click the drop-down box and select '**Green Fill with Dark Green Text'**

6. Click the '**OK**' button

7. Repeat **steps 1 & 2** above

8. This time select **Highlight Cells Rules : Less Than...**

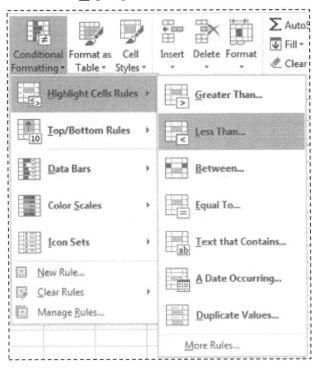

The following dialogue box should appear:

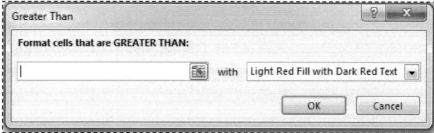

9. In the **'Format cells that are LESS THAN':** box enter **$1,000**

10. In the **'with':** box click the drop-down box and select '**Light Red Fill with Dark Red Text**'

11. Click the '**Ok**' button

12. Highlight columns **'A'** – **'D'**

13. From the toolbar select **DATA : Filter**

14. Click the filter drop-down arrow for **'TOTAL'** *(column 'D')*

15. Select **'Filter by Color'**

16. Select the green looking bar

You should see something similar to the following now being displayed.

	A	B	C	D
1	SALES PERSON FIRST NAM ▼	SALES PERSON LAST NAM ▼	QUARTER ▼	TOTAL ▼
9	Joe	Tanner	4	$ 39,631
13	Peter	Graham	4	$ 13,199
17	Helen	Simpson	4	$ 20,459
20	Alex	Steller	3	$ 13,431
21	Alex	Steller	4	$ 31,711
24	Billy	Winchester	3	$ 16,558

You've now identified the quarter and sales people with sales greater than $10,000.

---

1. Click the filter drop-down arrow for **'TOTAL'** *(column 'D')*
2. Select **'Filter by Color'**
3. Select the red looking bar

You should see something similar to the following now being displayed:

	A	B	C	D
1	SALES PERSON FIRST NAM ▼	SALES PERSON LAST NAM ▼	QUARTER ▼	TOTAL ▼
2	Jack	Smith	1	$ 343
6	Joe	Tanner	1	$ 377
10	Peter	Graham	1	$ 415
14	Helen	Simpson	1	$ 457
18	Alex	Steller	1	$ 502
22	Billy	Winchester	1	$ 552

You've now identified the quarter and sales people with sales less than $1,000.

To remove the Conditional Formatting:

1. From the toolbar select **HOME : Conditional Formatting:**

2. Select '**Clear Rules**' and either option:
   a. Clear Rules from <u>S</u>elect Cells
   b. Clear Rules from <u>E</u>ntire Sheet

FORMULA = LEN

Formula:
- LEN

Definition:
- Counts the number characters in a cell

Quick Example:

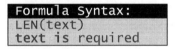

Formula Syntax:
LEN(text)
text is required

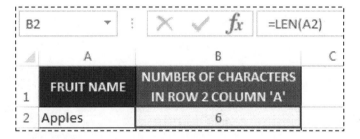

| B2 | ▼ | ⋮ | ✕ ✓ *fx* | =LEN(A2) |

◢	A	B	C
1	FRUIT NAME	NUMBER OF CHARACTERS IN ROW 2 COLUMN 'A'	
2	Apples	6	

Scenario:

You've been given a report that was created by a Database Administrator (DBA). The DBA created the file by running a query in a database, exporting the results into a .CSV file, and then opened and re-saved the report as an Excel® file.

As the Business Analyst, you're attempting to reconcile the data using a Pivot Table. In your analysis, you've discovered cell values that *"look"* to be the same, but are being returned as two separate records in your results.

You use the LEN function to troubleshoot why you're getting two separate records in your results for what appear to be the same value.

Detailed Example How To Use The Formula:

Sample data:

	A	B
1	**FRUIT NAME**	**FRUIT SALES**
2	Apples	100
3	Kiwi	100
4	Oranges	100
5	Apples	200
6	Kiwi	200
7	Oranges	200
8	Apples	300
9	Kiwi	300
10	Oranges	300
11		

Pivot table results, the fruit '**Apples**' is listed twice and should only be listed once:

	A	B
1		
2		
3	**Row Labels** ▾	**Sum of FRUIT SALES**
4	Apples	100
5	Apples	500
6	Kiwi	600
7	Oranges	600
8	**Grand Total**	**1800**
9		
10		

1. You begin by sorting the results by 'Fruit Name' in Ascending order

2. Add a column, in cell '**C1**' label it "**LEN FUNCTION**"

3. Next apply the '**LEN**' function for 'Fruit Name' in row '**C2**'

	A	B	C
1	FRUIT NAME	FRUIT SALES	LEN FUNCTION
2	Apples	100	
3	Apples	200	
4	Apples	300	
5	Kiwi	100	
6	Kiwi	200	
7	Kiwi	300	
8	Oranges	100	
9	Oranges	200	
10	Oranges	300	
11			

4. From the toolbar select **Formulas : Insert Function**

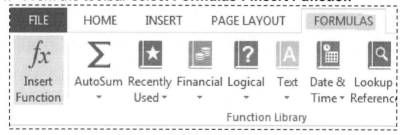

5. Type "**LEN**" in the **'Search for a function:'** dialogue box

6. Click the **'Go'** button

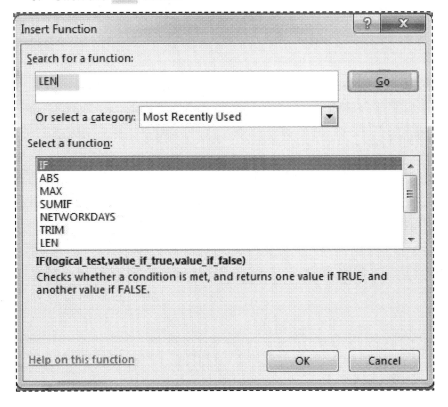

The following dialogue box should now appear:

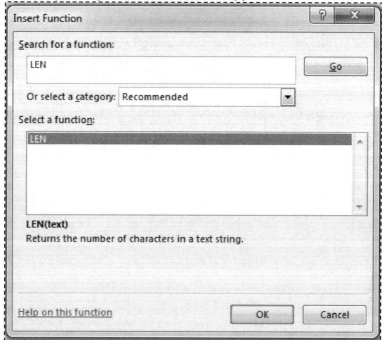

7. Click the '**OK**' button

8. Click on cell '**A2**' or enter '**A2**' in the dialogue box

9. Click 'the '**OK**' button

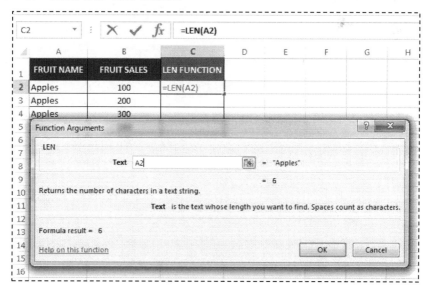

10. Copy the LEN formula down to cells '**C3**' thru '**C10**'

11. There appears to be an extra space in cells '**A3**' & '**A4**' for the fruit *'Apple'*

	A	B	C
1	**FRUIT NAME**	**FRUIT SALES**	**LEN FUNCTION**
2	Apples	100	6
3	Apples	200	7
4	Apples	300	7
5	Kiwi	100	4
6	Kiwi	200	4
7	Kiwi	300	4
8	Oranges	100	7
9	Oranges	200	7
10	Oranges	300	7

12. Remove the extra space in in cells '**A3**' & '**A4**' for the fruit 'Apple'

13. Save your changes

14. Re-run your Pivot Table

Results now appear correctly

3	**Row Labels** ▼	**Sum of FRUIT SALES**
4	Apples	600
5	Kiwi	600
6	Oranges	600
7	**Grand Total**	**1800**

FORMULA = TRIM

Formula:
- TRIM

Definition:
- Removes all extraneous spaces from a cell, except for single spaces between words.

Quick Example:

```
Formula Syntax:
TRIM(text)
text is required
```

C2	▼	:	✕ ✓	fx	=TRIM(A2)	

▲	A	B	C	D
1	FRUIT NAME	LEN COUNT OF CHARACTERS	TRIM FUNCTION	LEN COUNT OF CHARACTERS
2	Apples, Bananas, Mangos	27	Apples, Bananas, Mangos	23
3	Apples, Bananas, Mangos	23	Apples, Bananas, Mangos	23
4				

Scenario:

You've been given an Excel® report generated by another application. Upon review you see the content in some cells contains extra spaces between and after words. In order to make the report usable for analysis and presentation you need to remove the extraneous spaces.

Detailed Example How To Use The Formula:

Sample data:

	A	B
	FRUIT NAME	**LEN COUNT OF CHARACTERS**
1		
2	Apples, Bananas, Mangos	27
3	Apples, Bananas, Mangos	23
4	Kiwi, Oranges, Strawberries	27
5	Kiwi, Oranges, Strawberries	29
6	Blueberries, Raspberries, Blackberries	38
7	Blueberries, Raspberries, Blackberries	40

1. Add a column, in cell '**C1**' label it "**TRIM FUNCTION**"

2. Next, apply the '**TRIM**' function for 'Fruit Name' in row '**C2**'

	A	B	C
1	**FRUIT NAME**	**LEN COUNT OF CHARACTERS**	**TRIM FUNCTION**
2	Apples, Bananas, Mangos	27	
3	Apples, Bananas, Mangos	23	
4	Kiwi, Oranges, Strawberries	27	
5	Kiwi, Oranges, Strawberries	29	
6	Blueberries, Raspberries, Blackberries	38	
7	Blueberries, Raspberries, Blackberries	40	

3. From the toolbar select **Formulas : Insert Function**

4. Type "**TRIM**" in the **'Search for a function:'** dialogue box

5. Click the '**Go**' button

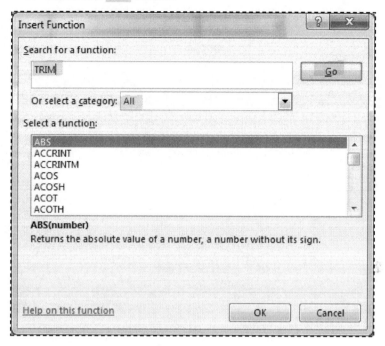

The following dialogue box should now appear:

6. Click the '**OK**' button

7. Click cell '**A2**' or enter '**A2**' in the dialogue box

8. Click the '**OK**' button

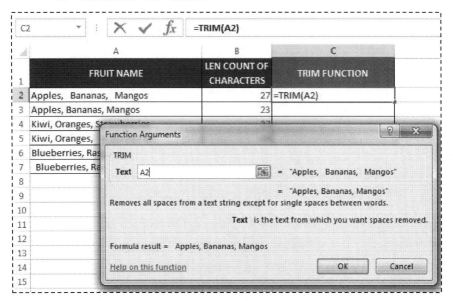

9. Copy the **TRIM** formula down cells '**C3**' thru '**C7**'

The extra spaces have been removed:

	A	B	C	D
1	FRUIT NAME	LEN COUNT OF CHARACTERS	TRIM FUNCTION	LEN COUNT OF CHARACTERS
2	Apples, Bananas, Mangos	27	Apples, Bananas, Mangos	23
3	Apples, Bananas, Mangos	23	Apples, Bananas, Mangos	23
4	Kiwi, Oranges, Strawberries	27	Kiwi, Oranges, Strawberries	27
5	Kiwi, Oranges, Strawberries	29	Kiwi, Oranges, Strawberries	27
6	Blueberries, Raspberries, Blackberries	38	Blueberries, Raspberries, Blackberries	38
7	Blueberries, Raspberries, Blackberries	40	Blueberries, Raspberries, Blackberries	38

*Next we'll copy and **paste as a values** the contents of **column C** and remove the columns (B, C, & D) that were used for troubleshooting.*

1. Highlight cells '**C2**' thru '**C7**'

2. Click the '**Copy**' button or **CTL+C** from your keyboard

3. Select cell '**A2**'

4. **Right click** and from the menu select '**Paste Special...**'

5. Select the '**Values**' radio button

6. Click the '**OK**' button

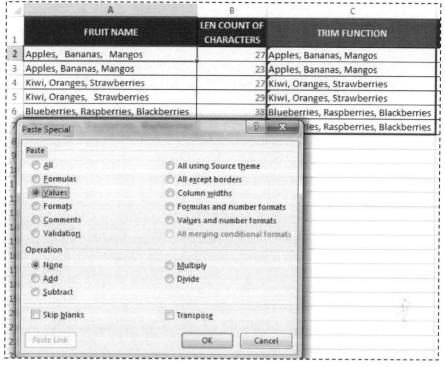

	A	B	C
1	FRUIT NAME	LEN COUNT OF CHARACTERS	TRIM FUNCTION
2	Apples, Bananas, Mangos	27	Apples, Bananas, Mangos
3	Apples, Bananas, Mangos	23	Apples, Bananas, Mangos
4	Kiwi, Oranges, Strawberries	27	Kiwi, Oranges, Strawberries
5	Kiwi, Oranges, Strawberries	29	Kiwi, Oranges, Strawberries
6	Blueberries, Raspberries, Blackberries	38	Blueberries, Raspberries, Blackberries
7			...ies, Raspberries, Blackberries

7. Highlight columns **'B'**, **'C'**, & **'D'**

8. **Right click** and select **'Delete'**,

The troubleshooting columns **'B'**, **'C'**, & **'D'** should now be removed

We have successfully removed all extraneous spaces from the values contained in **column 'A'**. Further analysis and reporting can be completed without error.

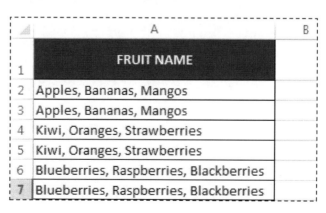

	A	B
1	FRUIT NAME	
2	Apples, Bananas, Mangos	
3	Apples, Bananas, Mangos	
4	Kiwi, Oranges, Strawberries	
5	Kiwi, Oranges, Strawberries	
6	Blueberries, Raspberries, Blackberries	
7	Blueberries, Raspberries, Blackberries	

FORMULAS = PROPER, UPPER, & LOWER

Formulas:
- PROPER, UPPER, & LOWER

Definition:

- **PROPER:** Converts the text of a cell to proper (normal case). The first letter of each word is uppercase (capitalized) and all other letters of the same word are lowercase.

- **UPPER:** Converts all text characters of a cell to **uppercase** (capitalized).

- **LOWER:** Converts all text characters of a cell to **lowercase.**

Quick Examples:

Formula Syntax:	Formula Syntax:	Formula Syntax:
PROPER(text)	UPPER(text)	LOWER(text)
text is required	text is required	text is required

	A	B	C
1	FROM--->	FORMULA	TO
2	apples	=PROPER(A2)	Apples
3	Apples	=UPPER(A3)	APPLES
4	APPLES	=LOWER(A4)	apples

Detailed Example How To Use The Formula:

Sample data:

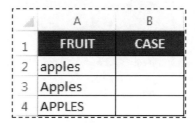

1. Place your cursor in cell **'B2'**

2. From the toolbar select **FORMULAS** and the **'Text'** drop-down box

3. For this example, select **'PROPER'**

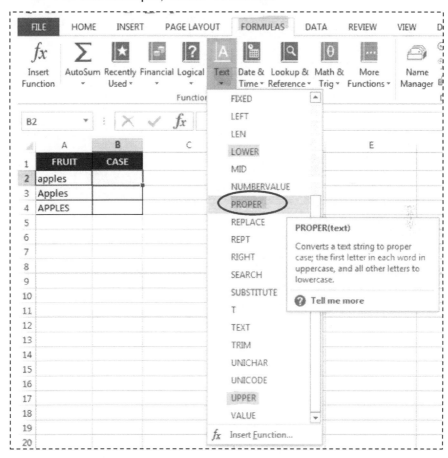

The following dialogue box should appear:

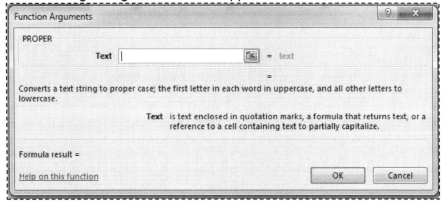

4. Click cell **'A2'** or enter **A2** in the **'Text'** box

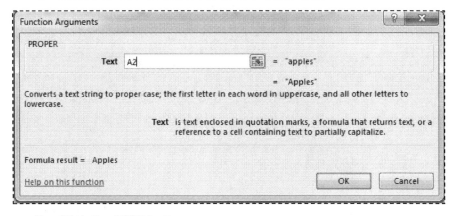

5. Click the **'OK'** button

The result should be as follows:

	A	B
1	FRUIT	CASE
2	apples	Apples
3	Apples	
4	APPLES	

You may copy the formula down to cells **'B3'** & **'B4'** or repeat the steps above and select a different option of **'UPPER'** or **'LOWER'** to practice using these formulas.

(PART 4) - CHAPTER 15
FORMULAS = CONCATENATE & MID

Formulas:
- CONCATENATE & MID

Definition:

- **CONCATENATE:** Joins two or more cells together and also allows the option to insert additional text into the merged cell.

- **MID:** Returns a specific number of characters from a text string, starting at the position you specify, based on the number of characters you stipulate.

Quick Examples:

```
Formula Syntax:
CONCATENATE(text)
text is required
```

	A	B	C	D
1	SALES PERSON FIRST NAME	SALES PERSON LAST NAME	FORMULA	Merged cells 'B2' & 'A2', Last Name, followed by a comma and space, then First Name
2	Jack	Smith	=CONCATENATE(B2,", ",A2)	Smith, Jack

```
Formula Syntax:
MID(text, start_num, num_chars)
All arguments are required
```

	A	B	C	D
1	SALES PERSON FIRST NAME	SALES PERSON LAST NAME	FORMULA	Started in positon 1 of cell 'A2' and returned the 1st character
2	Jack	Smith	=MID(A2,1,1)	J

Scenario for CONCATENATION:

You've been given a list of employees that need to be notified of a change in healthcare benefits. You've been asked to:

1. Generate an email list based on these names

Detailed Example How To Use The Formula:

Sample data:

	A	B
1	EMPLOYEE FIRST NAME	EMPLOYEE LAST NAME
2	Jack	Smith
3	Joe	Tanner
4	Peter	Graham
5	Helen	Simpson
6	Alex	Steller

1. Add a column, in cell **'C1'** label it "**EMAIL ADDRESS**"

2. Next, apply the '**CONCATENATION**' function for the Employee First & Last names to cell **'C2'**

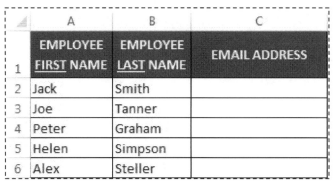

	A	B	C
1	EMPLOYEE FIRST NAME	EMPLOYEE LAST NAME	EMAIL ADDRESS
2	Jack	Smith	
3	Joe	Tanner	
4	Peter	Graham	
5	Helen	Simpson	
6	Alex	Steller	

3. From the toolbar select **FORMULAS** and the **'Text'** drop-down box

4. Select **'CONCATENATE'**

FILE	HOME	INSERT	PAGE LAYOUT	FORMULAS	DATA	REVIEW	VIEW

fx — Insert Function

Σ — AutoSum ▾

Recently Used ▾

Financial ▾

Logical ▾

Text ▾

Date & Time ▾

Lookup & Reference ▾

Math & Trig ▾

More Functions ▾

Name Manager

Function

| A1 | ▾ | : | ✕ | ✓ | *fx* | |

	A	B	C	D		G	H	I
1								
2								
3								
4								
5								
6								
7								
8								
9								
10								
11								
12								
13								
14								

Drop-down list:
BAHTTEXT
CHAR
CLEAN
CODE
CONCATENATE
DOLLAR
EXACT
FIND
FIXED
LEFT
LEN
LOWER
MID
NUMBERVALUE
PROPER

CONCATENATE(text1,text2,)
Joins several text strings into one text string.
? **Tell me more**

The following dialogue should now appear:

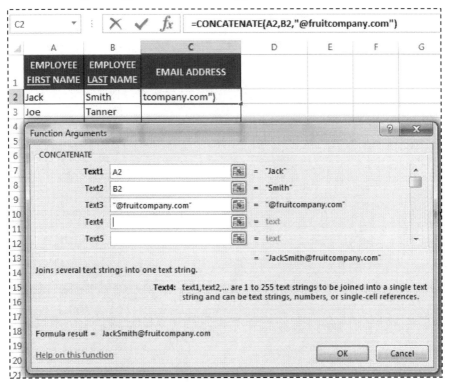

5. **Text1** box click cell '**A2**' or enter **A2**

6. **Text2** box click cell '**B2**' or enter **B2**

7. **Text3** box enter the text '**@fruitcompany.com**' *(you do not need to enter the quotation marks, these will be automatically added when using the formula wizard)*

8. Click the '**OK**' button

9. Copy the **CONCATENATE** formula down cells '**C3**' thru '**C6**'

C2	▼	:	×	✓	*fx*	=CONCATENATE(A2,B2,"@fruitcompany.com")		

◢	A	B	C	D	E
1	EMPLOYEE FIRST NAME	EMPLOYEE LAST NAME	EMAIL ADDRESS		
2	Jack	Smith	JackSmith@fruitcompany.com		
3	Joe	Tanner	JoeTanner@fruitcompany.com		
4	Peter	Graham	PeterGraham@fruitcompany.com		
5	Helen	Simpson	HelenSimpson@fruitcompany.com		
6	Alex	Steller	AlexSteller@fruitcompany.com		

We now have an email list.

Alternatively, we can perform the same type of functionality WITHOUT using the formula wizard for CONCATENATE. Instead, we can use the **ampersand (&) symbol**. This is how many intermediate and advanced Excel® users typically execute this command. Please see below for an example:

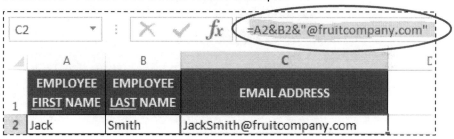

C2	▼	:	×	✓	*fx*	=A2&B2&"@fruitcompany.com"

◢	A	B	C	[
1	EMPLOYEE FIRST NAME	EMPLOYEE LAST NAME	EMAIL ADDRESS	
2	Jack	Smith	JackSmith@fruitcompany.com	

Scenario for MID

You've been given a list of stores from a database that prepends each location with three zeros. You need to pull information from this list into an existing spreadsheet that does not have the leading zeros for the stores. You plan on using the MID formula to:

1. Return the store number without the three leading zeros

Detailed Example How To Use The Formula:

Sample data:

	A	B
1	STORE NUMBER	NUMBER OF EMPLOYEES
2	000111	20
3	000222	27
4	000333	31
5	000444	18
6	000555	35

1. Add a column, in cell '**C1**' label it "**MID**"
2. Next, apply the '**MID**' function for the STORE NUMBER to cell '**C2**'

	A	B	C
1	STORE NUMBER	NUMBER OF EMPLOYEES	MID
2	000111	20	
3	000222	27	
4	000333	31	
5	000444	18	
6	000555	35	

1. From the toolbar select **FORMULAS** and the **'Text'** drop-down box

2. Select **'MID'**

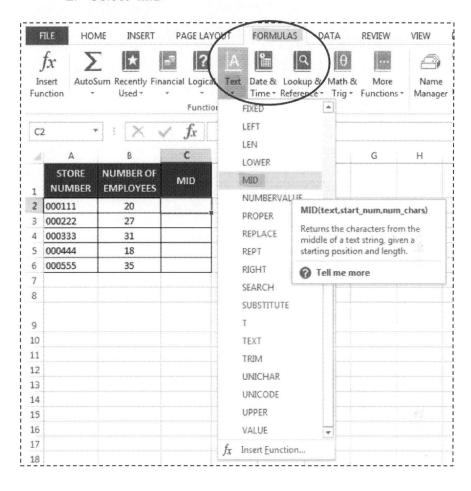

The following dialogue should now appear:

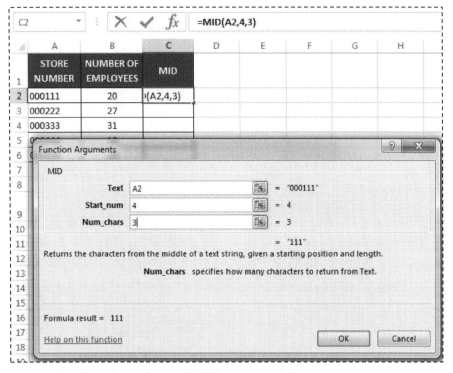

3. **Text** box click cell '**A2**' or enter **A2**

4. **Start_num** enter the number **4**, this is the position where the store number begins

5. **Num_chars** box enter the number **3**, this is the number of characters we want returned

6. Click the '**OK**' button

7. Copy the **MID** formula down cells '**C3**' thru '**C6**'

	A	B	C
1	STORE NUMBER	NUMBER OF EMPLOYEES	MID
2	000111	20	111
3	000222	27	222
4	000333	31	333
5	000444	18	444
6	000555	35	555

We now have a list of store numbers that do not contain the three leading zeros.

(PART 5) - CHAPTER 16
FORMULAS = IF & NESTED IF STATEMENTS

Formula:
- IF

Definition:
- IF formulas allow you test conditions and return one value *if true* and another *if false.*

- NESTED IF formulas allow you test conditions and return one value *if true* and another *if false*, if certain criteria is met.

Quick Example:

Formula Syntax:

IF(logical_test, value_if_true, [value_if_false])

logic_test required, value_if_true required, value_if_false optional

Basic IF formula:

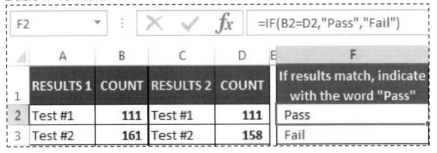

	A	B	C	D	E	F
F2					fx	=IF(B2=D2,"Pass","Fail")
1	RESULTS 1	COUNT	RESULTS 2	COUNT		If results match, indicate with the word "Pass"
2	Test #1	111	Test #1	111		Pass
3	Test #2	161	Test #2	158		Fail

Nested IF formula:

F4		✕ ✓ *fx*	=IF(B4=D4,"Pass",IF(B4-D4>5,"BIG FAIL","Fail"))		

	A	B	C	D	E	F
1	RESULTS 1	COUNT	RESULTS 2	COUNT		IF results match = **Pass** IF results DO NOT match = **Fail** IF results DO NOT match and the difference is greater than 5 = **BIG FAIL**
2	Test #1	111	Test #1	111		Pass
3	Test #2	161	Test #2	158		Fail
4	Test #3	183	Test #3	175		BIG FAIL
5	Test #4	243	Test #4	243		Pass
6	Test #5	263	Test #5	260		Fail

Scenario:

IF formulas are a very powerful tool for doing all types of analysis, let's walk through some examples:

1. You're a data analyst working on a project and need to compare test results

2. You've created a report and want a way to double check your formulas are calculating correctly

3. You need to evaluate if a sales person needs additional training based on their closing sales percentage

Detailed Example How To Use The Formula:

You're data analyst working on a project and need to compare test results.

1. If the results match between the two datasets, indicate with the word **'Pass'.**

2. If the results DO NOT match, show with the word **'Fail'.**

Sample Data:

	A	B	C	D	E	F
1	RESULTS 1	COUNT	RESULTS 2	COUNT		IF results match indicate with the word "Pass", otherwise label "Fail"
2	Test #1	111	Test #1	111		
3	Test #2	161	Test #2	158		
4	Test #3	183	Test #3	175		
5	Test #4	243	Test #4	243		
6	Test #5	263	Test #5	260		

1. Place your cursor in cell '**F2**'

2. From the toolbar select **Formulas : Insert Function**

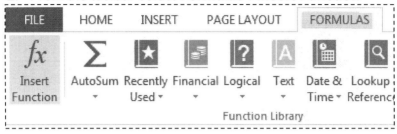

3. Type "**IF**" in the 'Search for a function:' dialogue box

4. Click the '**Go**' button

The following dialogue box should now appear:

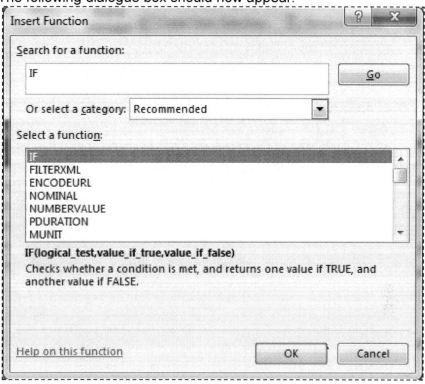

5. Click the '**OK**' button:
6. In the dialogue type the following:
   a. **Logical_test** = B2=D2
   b. **Value_if_true** = "Pass"
   c. **Value_if_false** = "Fail"

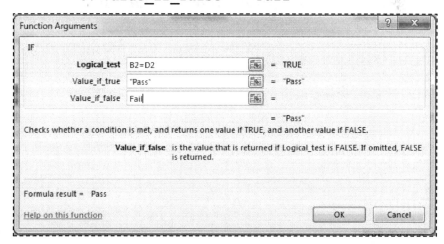

7. Click the '**OK**' button

8. Copy the formula to cells '**C3**' – '**C6**'

The result should look similar to the following, cell '**F2**':

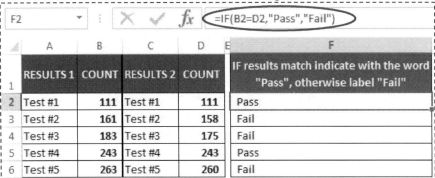

We've now compared two datasets and indicated if the results passed or failed.

Next scenario, you've created a report and want to verify the annual sales are correct.

We can accomplish this by summing the results of all the sales associates and comparing it to the total annual sales.

Sample data:

	ANNUAL SALES							
CURRENT YR	Q1	Q2	Q3	Q4	ANNUAL	SALES PERSON	SALES	
Actual Sales	$ 2,646	$ 23,586	$ 49,375	$ 107,505	$ 183,112	Graham, Peter	$22,708	
Percent of Sales	1.4%	12.9%	27.0%	58.7%		Simpson, Helen	$20,258	
						Smith, Jack	$10,339	
						Steller, Alex	$50,925	
						Tanner, Joe	$15,276	
						Winchester, Billy	$63,606	

1. Place your cursor in cell '**L6**'

2. From the toolbar select **FORMULAS** and the '**Logical**' drop-down box

3. Select '**IF**'

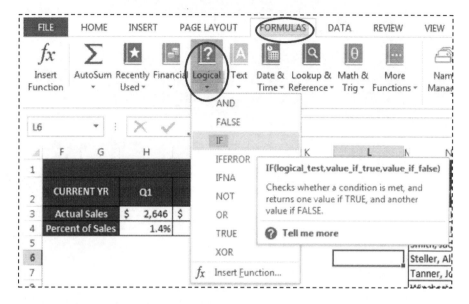

The following dialogue should now appear:

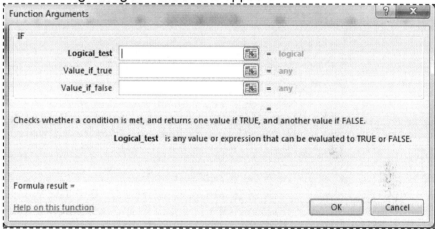

4. In the dialogue type the following:
   a. **Logical_test**   = SUM(O3:O8)=L3
   b. **Value_if_true** = Balance
   c. **Value_if_false** = Error in formula

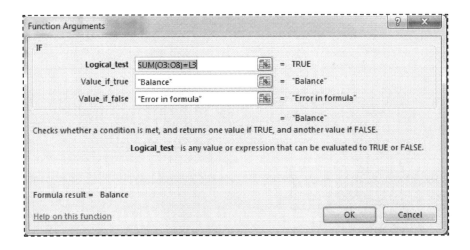

5. Click the '**OK**' button

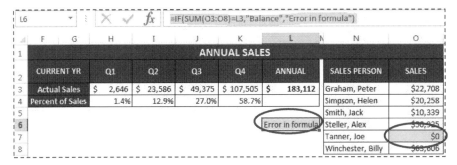

`=IF(SUM(O3:O8)=L3,"Balance","Error in formula")`

Our results balance, we've verified the annual sales are correct.

You can check the logic of the formula is working correctly, by changing a value for one of the sales people. **_NOTE:_** *how the formula now states "Error in formula."*

In our last example, we will examine **Nested IF** statements to determine, if a sales person needs additional training based on their closing sales percentage.

Using the associate's sales closing percentage, we will determine, if they are an "Achiever" and could mentor others. If the sales person is "Meeting expectations," or is falling behind and "Needs Additional Training." The criteria for our evaluation is as follows, for sales closing percent:

- 85% or higher = **Achiever**
- 70 – 84% = **Meeting Expectations**
- 69% or less = **Needs Training**

Unfortunately, the capabilities of the formula wizard do not extend very well for Nested IF functions. Therefore, I will breakdown the formula to describe how it works, basically we'll be entering a series of *If - Then statements*.

*Sample data **with results**:*

=IF(E3>=0.85,"Achiever",IF(E3>=0.7,"Meeting Expectations",IF(E3>=0.69,"Needs Training","Needs Training")))

D	E	F	G	H	I	J
SALES PERSON	% OF CLOSED SALES	85%< Achiever 70 - 84%> Meets Expectations 69%< Needs Additional Training				
Dower, John	60%	Needs Training				
Wilson, John	75%	Meeting Expectations				
Williams, Abbey	77%	Meeting Expectations				
Taylor, Sarah	70%	Meeting Expectations				
Graham, Peter	88%	Achiever				
Simpson, Helen	49%	Needs Training				
Smith, Jack	70%	Meeting Expectations				
Steller, Alex	85%	Achiever				
Tanner, Joe	80%	Meeting Expectations				
Winchester, Billy	66%	Needs Training				

A good way to start devising the formula is to write out your conditions using a format similar to the following:

❶ **IF** *column 'E' value is equal to or greater than 85%* **THEN** *Achiever*

❷ **IF** *column 'E' value is between 70-84%* **THEN** *Meeting Expectations*

❸ **IF** *column 'E' value equal to or less than 69%* **THEN** *Needs Training*

❹ **OTHERWISE** (all other closing percentages) *Needs Training*

In Excel®, these conditions represent a series of logic tests, with each being separated by a comma. Please see the illustration below.

1. Begin with your ❶ first IF condition and enter into cell **'F3'** as:
   - `=IF(E3>=0.85,"Achiever",` (**<u>NOTE:</u>** the comma)

2. Next, we add the ❷ second condition as:
   - `IF(E3>=0.7,"Meeting Expectations",`

3. The ❸ third IF condition:
   - `IF(E3>=0.69,"Needs Training",`

4. Lastly, the otherwise condition ❹:
   - `"Needs Training"`

5. Close the formula with four closing parenthesis **))))** as there were four conditions

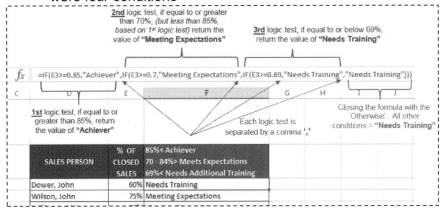

=IF(E3>=0.85,"Achiever",IF(E3>=0.7,"Meeting Expectations", ▲
IF(E3>=0.69,"Needs Training","Needs Training")))

```
=IF(E3>=0.85,"Achiever",IF(E3>=0.7,"Meeting
Expectations",IF(E3>=0.69,"Needs Training","Needs
Training")))
```

It can be a little confusing how you enter the percent conditions. As the second and third conditions (if statements) are being influenced by the preceding if condition.

For example, Excel® knows that '**E3>=0.7**' is really '**.70 - .84,**' because the preceding statement is '**E3>=0.85.**'

To finish copy the formula down to cells '**F4**' thru '**F12**' and you will have determined if a sales person needs additional training based on their closing sales percentage.

=IF(E3>=0.85,"Achiever",IF(E3>=0.7,"Meeting Expectations",IF(E3>=0.69,"Needs Training","Needs Training")))

D	E	F	G	H	I	J
SALES PERSON	% OF CLOSED SALES	85%< Achiever 70 - 84%> Meets Expectations 69%< Needs Additional Training				
Dower, John	60%	Needs Training				
Wilson, John	75%	Meeting Expectations				
Williams, Abbey	77%	Meeting Expectations				
Taylor, Sarah	70%	Meeting Expectations				
Graham, Peter	88%	Achiever				
Simpson, Helen	49%	Needs Training				
Smith, Jack	70%	Meeting Expectations				
Steller, Alex	85%	Achiever				
Tanner, Joe	80%	Meeting Expectations				
Winchester, Billy	66%	Needs Training				

(PART 5) - CHAPTER 17
FORMULA = VLOOKUP

Formula:
- VLOOKUP

Definition:
- The VLOOKUP formula allows you to search for and return a value from another Excel® list to a new Excel® list based on a matching lookup value.

Quick Example:

```
Formula Syntax:

VLOOKUP (lookup_value, table_array, col_index_num,
[range_lookup])


All parameters are required, except for
[range_lookup]
```

	A	B	C	D
1	SALES PERSON ID	SALES	VLOOKUP FORMULA	RESULT
2	200	469	=VLOOKUP(A2,Sheet2!A2:B6,2,FALSE)	Graham, Peter

The VLOOKUP formula is made-up of four parts:

❶ lookup value:

This is the field you want to find (match) typically located on another tab or spreadsheet.

In the example below, '**A2**' is selected which has the Sales Person ID value of '**200**'. I will look to match this value on the tab labeled '**Sheet2**'. Sales Person Name is the value I want to look-up and be returned to the tab labeled '**Sheet1**'.

❷ table array:

This is the spreadsheet (tab) and range of cells that are searched for the ❶ lookup_value. The field you want to match <u>must be</u> in the <u>first column</u> of the range of cells you specify in the ❷ table_array.

In the example below, I'm searching the tab labeled **'Sheet2'** with the cell range of **'A2:B6'**.

❸ col index num:

Is the column that contains the value you want returned.

In the example below, column **'2'** of the tab labeled **'Sheet2'** contains value of Sales Person Name that I want returned to the tab labeled **'Sheet1'**.

❹ range lookup:

Is the optional value of **'TRUE'** or **'FALSE'**. The value of **'FALSE'** would return an exact match, while **'TRUE'** would return an approximate match. Most users enter **'FALSE'** for this parameter.

Below, I have entered **'FALSE'** for an exact match.

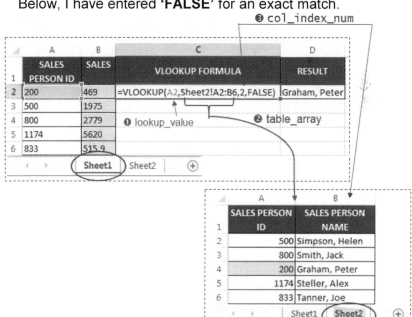

Scenario:

You've been asked to provide a list of the first quarter sales by month for each sales person. You run a query from the sales database and generate an Excel® report. Unfortunately, the database only contains the sales person's ID, but not their name. You use a VLOOKUP formula to pull the Sales Person's Name from an existing Excel® spreadsheet to the new sales report.

Detailed Example How To Use The Formula:

Sample data *(Sales Report with ID)*:

	A	B	C	D
1	SALES PERSON ID	Jan	Feb	Mar
2	200	$ 869	$ 1,092	$ 1,550
3	500	$ 1,975	$ 2,274	$ 2,719
4	800	$ 2,779	$ 3,002	$ 3,460
5	833	$ 7,716	$ 8,015	$ 8,460
6	1174	$ 5,620	$ 5,843	$ 6,301

Sheet1 | Sheet2 ⊕

Sample data *(Sales Person Name)*:

	A	B
1	SALES PERSON ID	SALES PERSON NAME
2	800	Smith, Jack
3	200	Graham, Peter
4	1174	Steller, Alex
5	500	Simpson, Helen
6	833	Tanner, Joe

Sheet1 | Sheet2 ⊕

1. On **'Sheet1'**, Insert a new column between columns **'A'** & **'B,'** label it "**SALES PERSON NAME**"

2. Next, apply the '**VLOOKUP**' formula for 'Sales Person Name' by clicking in cell '**B2**'

	A	B	C	D	E
1	SALES PERSON ID	SALES PERSON NAME	Jan	Feb	Mar
2	200		$ 869	$ 1,092	$ 1,550
3	500		$ 1,975	$ 2,274	$ 2,719
4	800		$ 2,779	$ 3,002	$ 3,460
5	833		$ 7,716	$ 8,015	$ 8,460
6	1174		$ 5,620	$ 5,843	$ 6,301

3. From the toolbar select **Formulas : Insert Function**

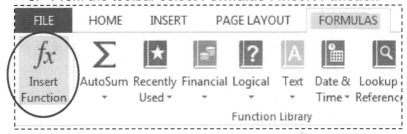

4. Type "**VLOOKUP**" in the **'Search for a function:'** dialogue box

5. Click the '**Go**' button

The following dialogue box should now appear:

6. Click the '**OK**' button

7. Click cell '**A2**' or enter **A2** in the dialogue box for the '**Lookup_value**' (the sales person ID is the field we'll lookup on '**Sheet2**')

8. For '**Table_array**', click on the tab '**Sheet2**' and highlight cells '**A2:B6**' this is the range of cells we're searching

9. Enter the number **2** for '**Col_index_num**' as this is the column with the sales person's name

10. For '**Range_lookup**' enter **FALSE**

11. Click the '**OK**' button

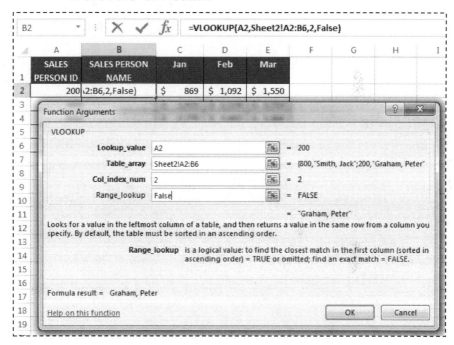

The following should be the result on **sheet1**:

B2	▼	:	✕ ✓ *fx*	=VLOOKUP(A2,Sheet2!A2:B6,2,FALSE)

▲	A	B	C	D	E	F
1	SALES PERSON ID	SALES PERSON NAME	Jan	Feb	Mar	
2	200	Graham, Peter	$ 869	$ 1,092	$ 1,550	
3	500		$ 1,975	$ 2,274	$ 2,719	
4	800		$ 2,779	$ 3,002	$ 3,460	
5	833		$ 7,716	$ 8,015	$ 8,460	
6	1174		$ 5,620	$ 5,843	$ 6,301	

12. We need to do one additional step before we can copy this formula down to cells '**B3**' thru '**B6**,' we must add the U.S. dollar symbol **$** to the **'Table_array'**. This will prevent our cell range from changing:

=VLOOKUP(A2,Sheet2!**$A$2:$B$6**,2,FALSE)

If we attempted to copy the VLOOKUP formula to cells '**B3**' thru '**B6**,' without adding the **$**, the result would be as follows, **_NOTE:_** *how the* **'Table_array'** *cell range changes:*

▲	A	B
1	SALES PERSON ID	SALES PERSON NAME
2	200	=VLOOKUP(A2,Sheet2!$A$2:$B$6,2,FALSE)
3	500	=VLOOKUP(A3,Sheet2!A3:B7,2,FALSE)
4	800	=VLOOKUP(A4,Sheet2!A4:B8,2,FALSE)
5	833	=VLOOKUP(A5,Sheet2!A5:B9,2,FALSE)
6	1174	=VLOOKUP(A6,Sheet2!A6:B10,2,FALSE)

We would also receive an error is cells '**B4**' & '**B6**'

▲	A	B	C	D	E
1	SALES PERS	SALES PERSON NAME	Jan	Feb	Mar
2	200	Graham, Peter	$ 869	$ 1,092	$ 1,550
3	500	Simpson, Helen	$ 1,975	$ 2,274	$ 2,719
4	800	#N/A	$ 2,779	$ 3,002	$ 3,460
5	833	Tanner, Joe	$ 7,716	$ 8,015	$ 8,460
6	1174	#N/A	$ 5,620	$ 5,843	$ 6,301

13. After adding the **$** to the **'Table_array'**, copy the
VLOOKUP formula to cells '**B3**' thru '**B6**'

We have successfully looked-up and added the Sales Person Name
to the quarterly sales report. We can now provide a list of the first
quarter sales by month for each sales person.

	A	B	C	D	E
1	SALES PERS	SALES PERSON NAME	Jan	Feb	Mar
2	200	Graham, Peter	$ 869	$ 1,092	$ 1,550
3	500	Simpson, Helen	$ 1,975	$ 2,274	$ 2,719
4	800	Smith, Jack	$ 2,779	$ 3,002	$ 3,460
5	833	Tanner, Joe	$ 7,716	$ 8,015	$ 8,460
6	1174	Steller, Alex	$ 5,620	$ 5,843	$ 6,301

Alternatively, for the **'Table_array'** you may enter the columns **A:B**
(Sheet2!A:B) instead of the range of cells (Sheet2!$A$2:$B$6),
if the *entire column* contains the data you want returned, this would
eliminate the need to complete **step 12**. However, depending on the
number of records you're looking up (the size of your data sample),
there could be a reduction in performance speed when selecting the
entire column, especially when using a combined formula, for
example a Nested IF and VLOOKUP function together.

Please see screenshots below for the complete example using
columns instead of a range of cells:

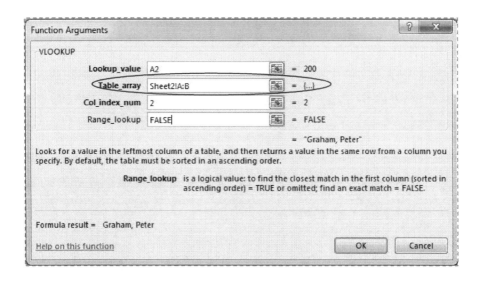

If you would like to learn more about the VLOOKUP formula, please check out my book: The Step-By-Step Guide To The **VLOOKUP** formula in Microsoft® Excel®

The book contains several more basic, intermediate, and advanced VLOOKUP examples with screenshots including how to:

- Incorporate the IFERROR functionality into your VLOOKUP formula

- How to apply the VLOOKUP formula across multiple tabs

- How to apply the VLOOKUP formula across multiple workbooks

In addition to the above, you will also learn how to **troubleshoot** and

resolve common VLOOKUP errors, that will **save you hours of frustration!**

- Reasons why you may be getting the **#N/A** error message
- Reasons why you may be getting the **#REF** error message
- Reasons why your VLOOKUP formula was working, but now you're getting the wrong values
- And more.....
-

CHAPTER 18
EXCEL® SHORTCUTS & TIPS

The following lists some of the most common Microsoft® Excel® shortcuts:

DESCRIPTION	COMMANDS
FORMATTING	
CTRL+B	Applies or removes **bold** formatting
CTRL+I	Applies or removes *italic* formatting
CTRL+U	Applies or removes underlining formatting
FUNCTION	
CTRL+A	Selects (highlights) the entire worksheet
CTRL+C	Copies the contents of selected (highlighted) cells
CTRL+X	Cuts the selected cells
CTRL+V	Pastes the contents of selected (highlighted) cells, including cell formatting
CTRL+F	Displays the Find and Replace dialog box, with the **Find** tab selected
CTRL+H	Displays the Find and Replace dialog box, with the **Replace** tab selected
CTRL+K	Displays the Insert Hyperlink dialog box for new hyperlinks or the Edit Hyperlink dialog box for selected existing hyperlinks
CTRL+N	Creates a new blank workbook
CTRL+O	Displays the dialog box to open a file
CTRL+S	Saves the active file with its current file name, location, and file format
CTRL+P	Displays the Print dialog box
CTRL+Z	The undo function will reverse the last command or to delete the last entry you typed
ESC	Cancels an entry in the active cell or 'Formula Bar'

NAVIGATION	
CTRL+PageUp	Switches between worksheet tabs, from **left-to-right**
CTRL+PageDown	Switches between worksheet tabs, from **right-to-left**
CTRL+↓	Goes to the last row with content for the active column
CTRL+↑	Goes to the first row with content for the active column
CTRL+→	Goes to the last column with content for the active row
CTRL+Home	Goes to cell A1 of the active worksheet
Shift + F3	Opens the Excel formula window
EDITING	
F7	Runs Spellcheck
Shift + F7	Opens the thesaurus dialogue box

☑ Helpful Tip:

Below are two ways to change a currency symbol. In the following examples, I will demonstrate the **British Pound £** and **Euro €**:

1. Select the cells you would like to change the currency, in this example, cells '**B2**' – '**B6**' are highlighted:

	A	B	C
1	US	British Pound	Euro
2	$ 100	100	100
3	$ 200	200	200
4	$ 300	300	300
5	$ 400	400	400
6	$ 500	500	500

2. From the '**HOME**' toolbar click the drop-down box for **$**

3. Select one of the currency's listed, in this example, '**£ English (United Kingdom)**' was selected

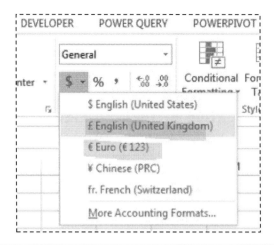

Alternatively, if your desired currency is not listed in the **'HOME'** toolbar **$** drop-down box, you can:

1. Select the cells you would like to change the currency

2. Right click and select **'Format Cells…'**:

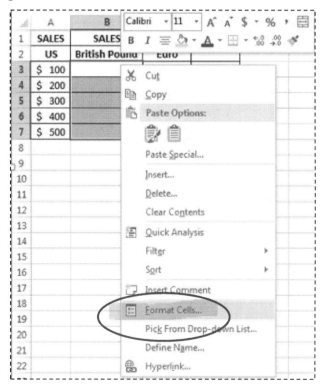

3. Select the tab **'Number'**

4. **'Category:' 'Currency'**

5. In the **'Symbol'** drop-down box select your desired currency, in this example, **'£ Engilsh (United Kingom)'** was selected:

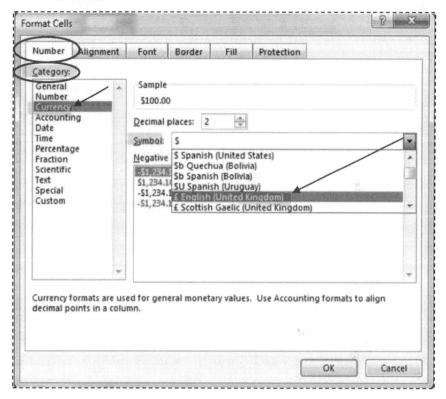

6. Click the **'OK'** button

7. Repeat the preferred method above, this time for the '**Euro €'** currency

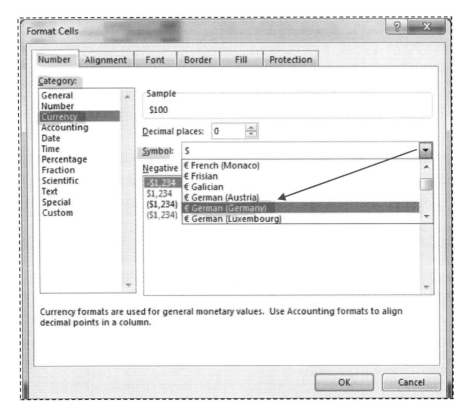

We now have currency displayed in the **British Pound £** and **Euro €**:

	A	B	C
1	US	British Pound	Euro
2	$ 100	£100	100 €
3	$ 200	£200	200 €
4	$ 300	£300	300 €
5	$ 400	£400	400 €
6	$ 500	£500	500 €

A Message From The Author

Thank you for purchasing and reading this book! Your feedback is valued and appreciated! Please take a few minutes and leave a review.

Other Books Available By This Author:

1. The Step-By-Step Guide To **Pivot Tables** & Introduction To **Dashboards**

2. The **Step-By-Step** Guide To The **VLOOKUP** formula in Microsoft® Excel®

3. The Microsoft® Excel® **Step-By-Step** Training Guide Book Bundle

Made in the USA
Middletown, DE
27 September 2017